PASTORAL MUSIC
IN PRACTICE
3

Initiation and Its Seasons

Edited by Virgil C. Funk

The Pastoral Press
Washington, D.C.

ISBN: 0-912405-74-0

The Pastoral Press
225 Sheridan Street, NW
Washington, D.C. 20011
(202)-723-1254

The Pastoral Press is the publications division of the National
Association of Pastoral Musicians, a membership organization of
musicians and clergy dedicated to fostering the art of musical
liturgy.

Printed in the United States of America

CONTENTS

INTRODUCTION

Few activities are more important to the Christian community than initiating its new members. By so doing the community not only ensures its survival into the future but also enriches its own inner spirit by sharing in the vision and faith experiences of those seeking membership. With the 1972 promulgation of the Rite of Christian Initiation of Adults (RCIA) we have come to learn that true initiation is embedded, not in theological indoctrination, but in shared reflection, support, prayer, and works of love. Undertaken by both those being initiated and by the initiating community, this step-by-step spiritual journey embodies that change of mind, heart, and outlook often referred to as conversion.

The various steps of this journey, as laid out in the RCIA, are marked by liturgical rites whose prayers and symbols express and intensify the individual's and the community's journey of faith. Signing with the cross, laying on of hands, the water bath, anointing with fragrant oil, sharing in the eucharistic bread and cup—all are vibrant and potent symbols of what is happening during this period of shared beginnings.

No less powerful is the role of ritual music throughout this initiatory journey. Pastoral musicians are beginning to discover that their ministry is crucial if the rites are to assume their hoped-for beauty, power, and efficacy. The faith and prayer of the church cannot be better proclaimed than in song, since well crafted melody and text engage participants on a unique level, one that penetrates to the depths of the human spirit. Pastoral musicians have admirably responded to the challenges of the revised order of Mass; now they are faced with a new challenge, that of enabling a initiatory community to celebrate and communicate its faith in song as it welcomes new members.

This volume gathers together some of the more significant articles on Christian initiation that have appeared within recent years in *Pastoral Music*, the membership journal of the National Association of Pastoral Musicians. Part One, "The Rites," presents a broad sketch of the theological, pastoral, and ritual dimensions of initiation. Part Two, "The Seasons," is a commentary on the Congregation for Divine Worship's 1988 circular letter on "Preparing and Celebrating the Paschal Feasts" (the full text of the letter is reproduced in an English translation prepared by the Vatican). This section is important because the major moments of initiation are not to be scattered willy-nilly throughout the year, but are intimately linked with the annual rhythms of Lent, the Triduum, and the season of Easter. Part Three, "The Music," offers the pastoral musician not only information on existing repertoire but also practical insights on how to enliven the musical moments of the rites so that all participating may together experience what it means to be a people who petition and praise the Lord in song.

Virgil C. Funk

THE RITES

Mark Searle

ONE

WELCOME YOUR CHILDREN
NEWBORN OF WATER

Twenty-five years ago, the idea of musicians being interested in baptism would have seemed unthinkable to all but a few avant-garde "litniks." It is an indication of how far we've come in rehabilitating Christian initiation to its proper place in the life of the church that pastoral musicians have now to consider how baptism may receive its full and proper musical celebration. However, the lack of a tradition of baptismal music means that a considerable creative effort is now needed and that effort, in turn, needs to be informed by a sound appreciation of the rich symbolism of the baptismal liturgy. It is the purpose of this article to review briefly the meaning of the baptismal rites in a way that may be helpful to musicians in writing music and planning celebrations for initiation.

TWO DISTINCT BAPTISMAL RITUALS

Given the particular focus of this article, we can leave aside several of the burning pastoral-theological issues such as who should be baptized, whether baptism should ever be deferred, the kind of preparation necessary for parents, the age at which the other initiatory sacraments should be celebrated, and so on. Nevertheless, it is impossible to think about the meaning of baptism without confronting the fact that in the Roman Church at present there exist two distinct rituals: the Rite for the Baptism of Children and the Rite for the Christian Initiation of Adults (RCIA). The reasons for this dichotomy are partly historical and partly pastoral.

Historically, the ritual of baptism developed as a ritual for the Christian initiation of adults. The rites were distributed over a period of time, running from entrance into the catechumenate at the beginning of Lent, through the scrutinies and exorcisms of the Sundays of Lent, to the proper climax in the celebration of baptism, confirmation, and eucharist at the conclusion of the Easter Vigil. During the period of the catechumenate, which is probably at the origin of Lent as we know it, there were daily instructions and prayers for those preparing for baptism; while after baptism, particularly in the first week of Easter, there was a kind of "debriefing" of the newly baptized, a period of "mystagogy" which was intended to help them appreciate more profoundly the mysteries into which they had been initiated.

Obviously, this practice was geared to the needs of adults converting to Christianity; but the children of such converts, as well as the children of the already baptized, were put through the same process. So much was this taken for granted that, when the number of adult converts tapered off and finally dwindled away, the same practices were retained for children almost without alteration. Efforts were made in some places to continue to celebrate the rites of initiation over a period of weeks, but when the instructions were dropped (for obvious reasons), and the catechumenate rites came to be celebrated outside the context of the Sunday assembly, all the rituals came to be condensed into a single, continuous, semiprivate ceremony. Whereas private baptism had hitherto been an exception in cases of emergency, the high infant mortality rate, together with the threat of loss of heaven implied in Augustine's association of infant baptism with original sin, led to it becoming the normal practice. This privatization of baptism, severing the sacrament from its communal context and from its place in the Easter Vigil, also meant that it was now habitually celebrated without the bishop being present. This, in turn, created the dilemma of what to do about the "sealing" or "confirming" of the newly baptized. Originally it had always been done by the bishop, as leader of the local community, immediately after the newly baptized had emerged dripping from the font and immediately before they participated, as infants or adults, in the celebration of the eucharist.

The consequences of these developments is the situation we have inherited. First, infants have been baptized for centuries with a ritual intended for adults and including elements such as solemn exorcisms and a first-person renunciation of Satan and profession of faith which which were clearly ill adapted to the condition of infancy. Second, the celebration of baptism—whether for infants or adults—became a private affair carried out in the absence not only of the bishop, but even of the local congregation. Third, the integral rite of initiation was broken up at the point where it could least afford to be broken up: at the very heart and climax of the process. If the catechumenal rites had been split up and separated from the baptismal liturgy by a longer or shorten period of time, no harm would have been done; but what happened was that the catechumenal rites were all lumped together while the water bath, the sealing with chrism, and the first act of communion were sundered from one another by a distance of several years. Confusion was further confounded when first communion was put before confirmation and the sacrament of penance was introduced to reconcile to the eucharistic table those who had never been admitted to it.

These problems were in the air on the eve of the Second Vatican Council, together with some urgent pastoral concerns. In mission territories with large numbers of adult converts the need was felt for an extended process of liturgical initiation. In post-Christian Europe, the practice of continuing to administer baptism to the children of nonpracticing parents was creating a situation in which baptism was little more than a social custom, more or less devoid of religious meaning. The council ordered a restoration of the catechumenate for the initiation of adult converts and mandated the preparation of a baptismal liturgy accommodated to the condition of young children and to the role of their families in their upbringing.

The effect of these reforms has been to promote a new sense of importance of baptism as the foundation of the Christian life, both individual and communal. No longer a hole-in-the-corner affair, baptism has emerged to take its proper place once again in the public life of the local church, whether at the Easter Vigil—its native habitat—or on various Sundays of the year in the setting of the parish assembly. Still, a number of problems remain unsolved, chiefly as the result of our inability to agree upon what is really involved in the Christian initiation of the children of believing parents. Discussion about the age for confirmation, its relation to first communion, and so on, are all symptomatic of that larger problem. Nevertheless, while the discussion continues and different kinds of experience are accumulated, we have, in fact, taken possession of two sets of initiatory ritual, each of which has much to say about the making of Christians and thus about the Christian life itself.

BAPTISM OF ADULTS

As has often been noted, there have been few postconciliar reforms with as much potential for transforming our common Christian life as the RCIA. Since its shape is described elsewhere, we can be content here merely to note what it contributes to an understanding of Christian baptism and Christian life and what sort of positive values it offers the musician.

In the first place, the most obvious feature of the RCIA is that it involves the local congregation in all sorts of different ways, not least liturgically. It would be quite impossible to celebrate it privately. At various stages, but especially on the Sundays of Lent, the catechumens play a central and highly visible role in the Sunday assembly. The same is true, after their baptism, on the Sundays of Easter. This says something significant about the congregation itself: what kind of community are we? We are speaking now, not in empirical terms, but in ideal ones. The rituals of the RCIA are full images of the local church as a holy people, a gathered community, those chosen and set apart, a sign to the world, a people who have passed through death to life in Christ, and so forth. The rites require and engender such self-awareness, and music will have a significant role in promoting it.

Second, the presence of the catechumens and neophytes in Lent and Easter respectively, gives a whole new dimension to these seasons. They are seen as *baptismal* seasons, as celebrations of the baptismal life, and hence as celebrations of the basics of Christian identity. In this way, we find ourselves celebrating during Lent and Easter not only what happens to the catechumens, not even what happened to Jesus and the disciples, but the meaning of our own lives as participation in the paschal mystery of death and resurrection. Confrontation with sin and death, with the demons of hopelessness and infidelity and indifference, gives way (for those who have made that confrontation) to the recognition in our midst of the one who was wounded and who now stands, and who holds the keys of life and death. What the musician, like the preacher, needs to do is discover the existential images in the Lent catechumenal liturgies and in those of Eastertide. This is done by reading the texts of the liturgy through the prism of the unfolding rites of initiation. Grasping those images, the musician gives the community the chance to appropriate them in song.

What the RCIA represents, then, is tangible evidence of God reconciling the world to himself through the mystery of Christ, dead and risen. The catechumens and neophytes are not only the actors, however; they mirror the continuing pattern of every Christian life. It is the recognition of this pattern of dying-in-order-to-live, refracted in so many diverse scriptural and liturgical images, that the musician will want to foster in the mood set and the words sung in the chants of the faithful.

BAPTISM OF INFANTS

The very success of the RCIA appears to be rendering the practice of baptizing infants somewhat problematic. Precisely because adult initiation is so moving, so profoundly rich in insight, it seems almost advisable to postpone baptism until the children are old enough to appreciate it. The debate is now engaged at various levels, but for the musician faced with the fact of infants being baptized the question is not so much whether it is pastorally advisable as what can be made of it liturgically. In actual fact, the rite for baptizing infants has a lot going for it, but it does need to be appreciated in more positive terms than the old "washing away of original sin."

The liturgy of infant baptism is in four simple parts: welcoming rites, liturgy of the word, liturgy of the sacrament, concluding rites. While it lacks the extended development which characterizes the RCIA, the impact of the RCIA has in fact helped us to appreciate some aspects of it which might otherwise have been neglected. For instance, it is a public rite, to be celebrated when as many of the local community as possible can be present. I once met a lovably eccentric priest who hoped that baptism could replace benediction in popular Catholic devotion. Since that seems unlikely to happen, the next best thing is what most parishes opt for: baptism at Sunday Mass. (It would be more helpful to think of it as a celebration of baptism, followed by celebration of eucharist, for the readings should be geared to baptism.) This in turn requires that certain Sundays in the year be chosen for the celebration of baptism, days already equipped with suitable readings; e.g., the baptism of the Lord, the Easter Vigil the Pentecost vigil, the patronal feast of the parish, Christ the King, or the feast of All Saints.

The trick is to view the texts of these feasts through the lens of baptism and to view baptism in the light of these texts. Failure to do this means a disjointed liturgy; attention to it will yield new insights into both sacrament and feast.

What is important is to seize upon the positive images which the rite of infant baptism offers. Whereas the RCIA grips us because of the profoundly moving presentation of the drama of breaking with the past and being delivered into new life, infants have no past of which to repent and remain (it is fervently hoped!) passive under the ministrations of the church. The musician in particular will want to pick up on the images of Christian life offered by the rite, the wonder of the mystery of our hidden life with God in the body of Christ which is the church. Sometimes, in reacting against the dismal and impoverished understanding of baptism which identified it just as the expurgation of original sin, we turn the celebration into an exuberant welcoming ceremony. That is all right as far as it goes, but the texts of the rite—and the symbols of water and chrism, light and robe—speak more profoundly of the kind of community we are. It would be a mistake to confuse the natural affection infants arouse with a profound sense of Christian identity. Especially helpful in this regard are the text provided for musical setting in the appendix of the rite (nos. 237–245). Here is just one example:

Holy Church of God, stretch out your hand
and welcome your children

newborn of water
and the Spirit of God.

In this and other texts, what is so rich are the images of the local church and the insights they provide into the mystery of our life together, which go far beyond the facile togetherness of calling ourselves a "parish family." Moreover, the images in the liturgy of infant baptism, especially those in the blessing of God over the font and the chant texts given in the appendix, highlight something which, in the sometimes grim adult struggle to be faithful, we sometimes overlook: the joy, the privilege, the hope that is ours as members of the community of the baptized.

The involvement of the musician in the celebration of baptism, then, is both a gauge of how far we have come and a pledge of a better future. Through attention to the baptismal imagery—which takes different and complementary forms in the adult and the infant rites—musical settings will contribute immensely, not merely to the proper celebration of the rites, but to our own sense of identity and vocation as a Christian people.

James B. Dunning

TWO

WHAT'S NEW ABOUT THE "NEW" RCIA?

The "old" Rite of Christian Initiation of Adults is not so very old; the provisional English translation came out in 1974. At that time Ralph Keifer insisted that the rite was so new and foreign to present practice that it was either suicide or prophecy of the highest order. We shall explore just what is so new (and so old) about that basic rite.

In 1986 the U.S. bishops approved a new translation of the rite that rearranged paragraphs so that the catechetical periods are now treated in tandem with the appropriate ritual celebrations. The bishops also included some American additions to the rite and set 1 September 1988 as the implementation date. We shall survey those additions.

What's Old about the RCIA?

To some people this new Catholic alphabet, RCIA, trumpets a distorted message; it sounds like one more program or organization like the CCD, *Renew*, or even NPM. No, the RCIA is a sacrament, the sacrament of initiation for adults. It is the church doing what makes us church—proclaiming and celebrating with new members the Good News of God's love in Christ Jesus. Like all the sacramental reforms since Vatican II, the RCIA reflects the council's vision of the church grounded in an older, more biblical identity of the church as community.

In that respect, the sacrament is much like music. Nations and religions pour their identity into song. Many biblical creeds of the early church were, in fact, hymns. Both the orthodox and heretics spread their message in song. The identity of a people runs through their folk music, through spirituals and cries for freedom like "We Shall Overcome." On the other hand, scripture scholar Walter Brueggemann insists that lack of singing is an index of exile from our roots and the loss of our identity. We are a people who scarcely sing—one sign that we have forgotten who we are: a people loved by God with something to sing about.

Vatican II reminded us who we are. When bishops arrived at the council, they received a draft constitution on the church with an opening chapter on the hierarchy. They changed that and put first things first—a chapter on the mystery of God's presence in the church, then a chapter on the people of God, then a chapter on the hierarchy. The council offered us a biblical vision on the entire body of Christ, gifted by the Spirit as "a chosen race, a royal priesthood, a holy nation, a purchased people" (1 Pt 2:9).

The RCIA is the sacrament of initiation into that people. When groups initiate members, they tell people who they are; they raise basic questions of identity. What is oldest and newest about this sacrament of initiation is its ecclesiology, its vision of the church, its return to an identity that calls all members to active witness and mission. This sacrament includes all the baptized in the very mission of initiating: "The people of God, as represented by the local Church, should understand and show by their concern that the initiation of adults is the responsibility of all the baptized."[1] The first ministry listed for the RCIA is that of the entire community. The text then names a myriad of ministries within that community: sponsors, godparents, the bishop, priests, deacons, catechists.

Keifer could insist that this vision might be suicide because it raises challenges experienced since Vatican II about shared ministries. It assumes a community ready to witness to faith, and it assumes that this community forms new members for witness and mission. Although converts often became active members in the old system of inquiry classes, that system assumed a vision of the church and conversion captured in the title of a catechism,

Father Smith Instructs Jackson. The church was the priest; conversion was about Catholic knowledge; Jackson was the passive receiver.

The RCIA assumes that the church is the community; conversion is about head, heart, and hands; and Jackson actively witnesses his or her faith to the parish during and after initiation. This vision can be so far from the reality that Regis Duffy claims that some parishes aren't worthy of joining and shouldn't touch the RCIA. I suggest that just as babies can renew and change a family, so the "babies" called catechumens by their faith and new life can renew tired old Catholics and teach us how to sing.

That is why rites and music in the rites are so basic to the community's welcome to catechumens. The liturgical assembly is the parish's prime time to celebrate Good News, and as much as anything, music is that assembly's way of doing it. When the assembly sings its identity as a community of disciples and missionaries, that is "prophecy of the highest order."

So What's New?

Rooted in that vision of the church, what other challenges does the celebration of this sacrament offer? First, more than other rites, the RCIA sees "sacrament" as a journey punctuated by liturgies and not as a one-time event or magic moment (e.g., pouring water, exchanging vows). This sacrament offers a galaxy of celebrations signifying welcome by the parish and inclusion: signing the senses, pondering God's word, blessings, witness by the godparents, signing the Book of the Elect, laying on hands, immersing, anointing, eating and drinking. In a Spirit-filled community God is present throughout this journey. This sounds the death knell to terminal sacramental preparation programs and one-time-born-again conversions. In a sense, this sacrament never ends. Eucharist is the repeatable sacrament of initiation, and conversion is a lifelong journey celebrated again and again at the eucharist.

Second, evangelization (aimed at initial conversion) and catechesis (aimed at deepening conversion) never address only the brain's cortex. Some people may think that conversion is only a matter of changing churches or learning a particular church's doctrines. In the past, "inquiry classes" often offered theology and interesting information, but not personal transformation into Jesus Christ.

The RCIA invites a person "to feel called away from sin and drawn into the mystery of God's love" in "a relationship with God in Christ."[2] We can't assume this experience of God's love even in the baptized. In a Gallup study of all the churches, Catholics were the least likely respondents to agree that "God loves me a great deal" and "I have a personal relationship with God." In another study, thirty-eight percent of priests identified faith with accepting doctrine, not with relationship with God. If the latter is the goal, then RCIA sessions that explore this relationship in people's experience are more like AA meetings, where all members share their stories. Then we connect our personal stories to the great stories of Scripture. Indeed doctrine has a place, but it flows from life and gives meaning to life, like AA's doctrine of the twelve steps.

Third, this sacrament needs catechesis and liturgy, word and rite. In the past, initiation often consisted of privatized events taking place in the dark vestibule of a church, with no one present but the immediate family. Now the sessions lead into and flow from communal celebrations. The principal catechesis is set within the Sunday liturgy of the word, followed by the invitation to leave after the homily for reflection on and feasting at the table of the word, until the catechumens are ready to come to the table of the eucharist. The rites themselves communicate the Good News and the meaning of initiation and conversion.[3] Also, unlike theology classes, catechesis shares the qualities of good liturgy, for example, using more images than concepts, more stories than philosophizing, aiming more for the combination of head, heart, and hands than merely for the cortex, more communal than private, more prayer and music than lecture.

An American RCIA?

There is some unofficial bad news and some official good news about the American adaptation of the RCIA. The bad news is not in the rite but in what some programmatic Americans do to the rite. Those who used to identify conversion with religious knowledge and covering chapters in a catechism would program inquiry classes into neat, predetermined curricula with a fixed calendar (often three months). They see that the RCIA is more complex, so they extend the time to accord with the nine-month school year (because everything in America happens then)! Everybody starts the catechumenate in September, and they all end in May, with initiation seen as graduation rather than as a launching pad for mission. Parishes that see conversion as personal surrender to the Lord, which cannot be programmed, on the other hand, welcome inquirers at any time of the year, tailor the journey (short or long) to the needs of the person, and schedule many interviews and offer sponsors to meet those diverse personal needs.

The good news consists of the additions to the official American version of the sacrament. The 1974 interim text included baptized but uncatechized adults in the RCIA. Notice that the adjective is not "untheologized" or "uninstructed," but "uncatechized": the person has not personally heard the Good News as described above. Most inquirers in North America are not unbaptized catechumens but baptized Christians seeking full communion in our church. Some come strong in faith; they may not need evangelization, but they may need some time for answering questions about the Catholic Church and being integrated into parish life.

We do not assume, however, that the baptized are catechized. The person may have had little or no contact with a community of faith or may have been exposed only to the externals of religion. Therefore, in Part II of the new RCIA, the American bishops added a Rite of Election for children of catechetical age and four celebrations for baptized adults similar to those for unbaptized catechumens. In Appendix I they added four combined rites for joint celebrations with the unbaptized and the baptized. These additions respect pastoral sensitivity for baptized candidates, because they need to celebrate what is often a profound experience of conversion. The new texts also reflect ecumenical sensitivity, because the rites for the baptized use language that honors their baptism.

That is what is new about the RCIA. What is old is that people who discover who they are, a people called and gifted by God, always need to sing in thanksgiving about who they are and in praise of who their God is.

Notes

1. English translation of the Rite of Christian Initiation of Adults, 1988, Introduction no. 9 (in the interim version, 1974, this is no. 41. The final text rearranges the paragraphs of the Introduction.)

2. RCIA no. 37 (interim version, no. 10) and no 42 (interim version, no. 15).

3. See RCIA no. 75–3 (interim version, no. 19–3).

Robert J. Kennedy

THREE

THE DILEMMA OF CONFIRMATION

Anyone who is even casually acquainted with the pastoral questions that surround confirmation would do well to heed all warning signs. The watchword is "Stay away or be forever caught," for the way out is a dense and tangled path. But there are plenty of fools who wish to brave the wilds, so in we go!

The tangle is at the point where theology meets pastoral practice. To what is confirmation connected? How does it fit into the sacramental life of Christians? An examination of the present practice of confirmation in general terms will lead to the theology it reflects, and in turn will raise some major questions that bear upon pastoral practice.

The sacramental practice of confirmation today can be characterized as varied, uncertain, and unsettled. Preparation programs range in length from one or two sessions to two years or longer. The content of this formation is sometimes as narrow as the instruction on the sacrament alone (one wonders what is said!), and sometimes as broad as a full review of Christian doctrine. And a survey of the dioceses in the United States reveals that confirmation is given at almost every age between infancy and seventeen.

Of course, the question of age is the most burning practical question regarding confirmation today. (This is certainly not the most *important* question, however.) Again, the survey revealed

17

that, while the range of age is so great, the larger number of dioceses celebrate confirmation at the junior high school level (11-14 years old), with some movement toward the senior high school level (15-17 years old). This is significant because it reflects a particular theological understanding of confirmation.

It is an understanding of confirmation that John Roberto (in his excellent NCCD Resource Paper, "Confirmation in the American Catholic Church") characterizes as the "theological-maturity school of thought." In summarizing this approach to the sacrament, he describes confirmation as "the rite of passage into Christian adulthood, the celebration of Christian maturity, the sacrament of witness and Christian mission, a time for decision, choice and commitment . . . the strengthening of the Spirit for mission, the communication of the grace of Pentecost, and the conferral of the full rights of membership in the faith community" (p. 22).

Anyone who has been involved with confirmation preparation at the junior and senior high school levels knows the elements of this summary well. They have been the substance of the instruction, retreat days, service projects, and liturgical rites that are part of the formation. But there are problems.

Problems

First, there is a pastoral problem. There is an inherent contradiction in the idea of linking maturity, adult mission, and participation—absolutely fluid qualities—to specific age or grade levels. The logical outcome of the maturity school of thought should be a provision that the reception of confirmation be open-ended, determined by the choice of the candidate and not the parish staff, religious education director, or parents. This could occur at age 7 or 77, depending on the discernment of the candidate; when choice, maturity, and commitment are the ideals, no age can be determined in advance. And, because maturing is a lifelong process, wouldn't it also be logical to celebrate confirmation more than once in a lifetime, when a person comes to new and deeper levels of Christian maturity?

Second, there is a psychological/spiritual problem. Adolescence is probably the worst time to think about a commitment and to make choices. One youth minister recently observed that he believed the souls of teenagers went into hibernation during these years; to speak of God or Christ at this time in their lives was useless until they were well through the processes of physical and emotional growth and socialization. This is not to say that the church and all its ministries should abstain from caring for these young people. The opposite is especially important at this time. The real question is whether this is the time to speak of maturity, commitment, and adult responsibility for Christian mission. What, after all, do we mean by maturity?

Third, and most important, there is a theological problem. If confirmation is a sacrament of faith commitment and mission, what is required for baptism? If confirmation is the conferral of the grace of Pentecost, how can baptism be understood apart from the presence and activity of the Holy Spirit? And to speak as though confirmation conferred full rights of membership in the church is to deny baptism any value at all.

In short, the theological problem of the "maturity approach" is its negligence of "the intimate connection (of confirmation) with the whole of Christian initiation" (Constitution on the Sacred Liturgy no. 71). Apart from a close and obvious relationship with baptism and the eucharist, confirmation flounders for meaning. It is either understood as part of Christian initiation, or its meaning is concocted. And this is precisely the dilemma: the connection of present pastoral practice with a theology of initiation.

One might wonder: why worry about it? Confirmation has a good theology now, one that fits the particular needs of our time, and it keeps our children coming to religious instructions. This ignores that the tradition of the church and the restored and revised rites of Christian initiation see confirmation as integral to the initiation process, and not as a question of maturity. And if one is using confirmation to "keep 'em coming to class," something is seriously wrong already.

A Theological Vision

The Roman documentation on initiation—the Rite of Christian Initiation of Adults (1972), the Rite of Baptism for Children, with its introductory essay entitled "Christian Initiation" (1969), and the Rite of Confirmation (1971)—makes three concepts absolutely clear: 1) the sacraments of baptism, confirmation, and eucharist constitute the rite of Christian initiation; 2) there is an organic unity among these sacraments; and 3) the presumed, preferred, and normal order of the sacraments of initiation is baptism, confirmation, and eucharist. These concepts may seem radically new to those who were schooled to believe that confirmation made one a "soldier of Christ," ready for Christian adulthood. But in fact these thoughts are very old, reaching back to earlier practice and understanding, as do the revised rites themselves. The restoration of the liturgy of Christian initiation, based on the rich tradition of the church, has established that confirmation is an integral part of the initiation rite. Separate celebrations and/or an inverted order of the sacraments must be considered an abnormal practice.

But why? What are the theological foundations of confirmation? If the Constitution on the Sacred Liturgy speaks of "the intimate connection" of confirmation with the whole of Christian initiation, this is not simply wishful thinking, but a solid theological call.

The emphasis of any theology of confirmation is the reception of the Spirit, but within a broad scriptural context. When Christ was baptized, the Spirit came upon him (Mk 1:10 and parallels), he began his mission under the impulse of the Spirit (Lk 4:17–21), and he promised the Spirit to the apostles that they might bear witness to the faith before persecutors (Lk 12:12). In Acts of the Apostles (19:1–6) Paul, in response to the fact that some Ephesian disciples had "not so much as heard that there is a Holy Spirit," *baptized* them in the name of the Lord Jesus. Then, "as Paul laid his hands on them, the Holy Spirit came down on them." While one should be hesitant to deduce a specific or set liturgical/catechetical practice from the scriptural data, it is clear that baptism and the gift of the Spirit are intimately bound together as two aspects of the single reality of becoming Christian.

This is likewise reflected in the present documentation: "Through the sacraments of Christian initiation men and women are freed from the power of darkness. With Christ they die, are buried and rise again. They receive the Spirit of adoption which makes them God's sons and daughters and, with the entire people of God, they celebrate the memorial of the Lord's death and resurrection" ("Christian Initiation," no. 3).

Thus, it is imperative that confirmation be understood, in pastoral practice and theology alike, in its intimate connection with the whole process of initiation. It is the only way in which it has any sensible meaning.

But here is the crux of the dilemma: how can sound pastoral practice be built upon this sound initiation theology? The answer takes us to the rite of Christian initiation of adults, which should be seen as the normative procedure for initiation, that is, for making people Christian. This rite presupposes that becoming Christian is a process of growth, a spiritual journey that takes place step by step in the midst of the community of the faithful. Each person cooperates with God's grace in a unique way and moves toward full initiation (baptism, confirmation, eucharist) as faith and conversion mature and deepen in one's life.

Practical Steps

For the practice of confirmation to be accommodated to this vision and norm, the following steps must be taken quickly and consistently.

First, all who have not received the three sacraments of initiation are still to be considered catechumens. Thus, until all three are celebrated, the formation period should be governed throughout by the principles of the catechumenate (RCIA, no. 19), the overriding purpose of which is to bring to maturity the seedling faith of the initial conversion and to assist the candidates in living in the Christian way. Confirmation will then be deeply related to baptism and seen as an extension and completion of it. "Confirmation programs" will be refocused toward deeper faith formation and spiritual direction, and at living in the church community.

Second, while this sounds very much like the maturity-commitment school of thought, it is not. Confirmation by the model of the catechumenate will carry the sense of beginning, of commencement in the lifelong task of growing into Christ, and not of graduation from church practice, as so frequently seems to be the case today. Therefore, candidates for the completion of initiation should be only those who are elected for that completion. In other words, not all who are catechumens will move toward full initiation at the same pace, and that should be respected. God's grace works uniquely in each candidate, family, and community. Some, in the end, will and indeed should choose not to complete their initiation.

Third, in order to respect this activity of the Spirit of God—and in order to restore the integrity and organic unity of the sacrament of initiation—the celebration of confirmation will have to be removed from any particular age or grade. For the time being, confirmation should not be moved to before first communion (see Rite of Confirmation, no. 11), because we are not ready for that move, and, more important, because we need to get a firm hold on the catechumenal formation of candidates. This hold may pry baptism loose from infancy, and may allow the reunion of baptism and confirmation in a single rite later in childhood, adolescence, or, who knows, maybe even adulthood.

Fourth, bishops must assume strong leadership in the move to base confirmation on initiation theology. They must thoroughly study the rites themselves and their inherent theology, and encourage that study throughout their dioceses. They must take seriously their role in the process of Christian initiation, and whenever they preach at the full rites of initiation or the separate rites of baptism, confirmation, and first eucharist, they must open the word to all present in terms of baptismal responsibility for and participation in the Christian life. Bishops, for the sake of preserving and restoring the process of initiation, must ask for the appropriate indults from Rome to allow priests to confirm more regularly than they do. It is more important that initiation into the Christian community be presented and celebrated as a single, unified process than that the bishop come to confirm. Initiation *originates* from him (Rite of Christian Initiation of Adults, no. 7), but is shared by him with priests and deacons.

Finally, every parish community must take responsibility for bringing in better alignment the pastoral practice of confirmation and the rites and traditions of the church. Preaching must provide the "baptismal therapy" so desperately needed by the majority of our faithful people, a breaking open of the word so that faith will be nourished and people will turn more and more to the way of Christ. Catechesis at every level, from prebaptismal programs to adult education, should not be an intellectual pursuit alone; it should be aimed at the development of the whole Christian person. Above all, good liturgical celebrations should be planned so as to foster and nourish faith in all the congregation (see Music in Catholic Worship, nos. 6–9).

This last point about parish renewal would seem to move us very far from the discussion about putting confirmation in its place, but this is not so. Confirmation will recover its proper place when we have, as a church, diocese, and parish, come to terms with our baptism, the commitment in faith it entails, the participation in church life it demands, the living of the gospel life it requires, and the joy and gratitude it enables.

THE SEASONS

PREPARING AND CELEBRATING THE PASCHAL FEASTS

Preface

1. The Easter solemnity, revised and restored by Pius XII in 1951, and then the Order of Holy Week in 1955 were favorably received by the church of the Roman rite.[1]

The Second Vatican Council, especially in the Constitution on the Sacred Liturgy, repeatedly drawing upon tradition, called attention to Christ's paschal mystery and pointed out that it is the fount from which all sacraments and sacramentals draw their power.[2]

2. Just as the week has its beginning and climax in the celebration of Sunday, which always has a paschal character, so the summit of the whole liturgical year is in the sacred Easter triduum of the passion and resurrection of the Lord,[3] which is prepared for by the period of Lent and prolonged for 50 days.

3. In many parts of the Christian world the faithful followers of Christ, with their pastors, attach great importance to the celebration of this rite and participate in it with great spiritual gain.

However, in some areas where initially the reform of the Easter Vigil was received enthusiastically it would appear that with the passage of time this enthusiasm has begun to wane. The very concept of the vigil has almost come to be forgotten in some places, with the result that it is celebrated as if it were an evening Mass, in the same way and at the same time as the Mass celebrated on Saturday evening in anticipation of the Sunday.

27

It also happens that the celebrations of the triduum are not held at the correct times. This is because certain devotions and pious exercises are held at more convenient times, and so the faithful participate in them rather than in the liturgical celebrations.

Without any doubt, one of the principal reasons for this state of affairs is the inadequate formation given to the clergy and the faithful regarding the paschal mystery as the center of the liturgical year and of Christian life.[4]

4. The holiday period which today in many places coincides with Holy Week and certain attitudes held by present-day society concur to present difficulties for the faithful to participate in these celebrations.

5. With these points in mind, the Congregation for Divine Worship, after due consideration, thinks that it is a fitting moment to recall certain elements, doctrinal and pastoral, and various norms which have already been published concerning Holy Week. All those details which are given in the liturgical books concerning Lent, Holy Week, the Easter triduum and paschal time retain their full force unless otherwise stated in this document.

It is the aim of this document that the great mystery of our redemption be celebrated in the best possible way so that the faithful may participate in it with ever greater spiritual advantage.[5]

I. Lenten Season

6. "The annual Lenten season is the fitting time to climb the holy mountain of Easter.

The Lenten season has a double character, namely to prepare both catechumens and faithful to celebrate the paschal mystery. The catechumens, both with the rite of election and scrutinies and by catechesis, are prepared for the celebration of the sacraments of Christian initiation; the faithful, ever more attentive to the word of God and prayer, prepare themselves by penance for the renewal of their baptismal promises."[6]

a) Concerning the Rite of Christian Initiation

7. The whole rite of Christian initiation has a markedly paschal character, since it is therein that the sacramental participation in

the death and resurrection of Christ takes place for the first time. Therefore Lent should have its full character as a time of purification and enlightenment, especially through the scrutinies and by the presentations; naturally the paschal vigil should be regarded as the proper time to celebrate the sacraments of initiation.[7]

8. Communities that do not have any catechumens should not however fail to pray for those who in the forthcoming paschal vigil will receive the sacraments of Christian initiation. Pastors should draw the attention of the faithful to those moments of significant importance to their spiritual life nourished by their baptismal profession of faith, and which they will be invited to renew in the Easter Vigil, "the fullness of the Lenten observance."[8]

9. In Lent there should be catechesis for those adults who, although baptized when infants, were not brought up in the faith and consequently have not been confirmed nor have they received the eucharist. During this period, penitential services should be arranged to help prepare them for the sacrament of reconciliation.[9]

10. The Lenten season is also an appropriate time for the celebration of penitential rites on the model of the scrutinies for unbaptized children who are at an age to be catechized, and also for children already baptized, before being admitted to the sacrament of penance.[10]

The bishop should have particular care to foster the catechumenate of both adults and children, and, according to circumstances, to preside at the prescribed rites, with the devout participation of the local community.[11]

b) Celebrations During the Lenten Season

11. The Sundays of Lent take precedence over all feasts and all solemnities. Solemnities occurring on these Sundays are observed on the preceding Saturday.[12] The weekdays of Lent have precedence over obligatory memorials.[13]

12. The catechesis on the paschal mystery and the sacraments should be given a special place in the Sunday homilies; the text of the Lectionary should be carefully explained, particularly the passages of the Gospel which illustrate the diverse aspects of baptism and of the other sacraments, and of the mercy of God.

13. Pastors should frequently and as fully as possible explain the word of God in homilies on weekdays, in celebrations of the word of God, in penitential celebrations,[14] in various reunions, in visiting families or on the occasion of blessing families. The faithful should try and attend weekday Mass, and where this is not possible, they should at least be encouraged to read the lessons, either with their family or in private.

14. "The Lenten season should retain something of its penitential character."[15] "As regards catechesis, it is important to impress on the minds of the faithful not only the social consequences of sin, but also that aspect of the virtue of penance which involves the detestation of sin as an offense against God."[16]

The virtue and practice of penance form a necessary part of the preparation for Easter. From that inner conversion of heart should spring the practice of penance, both for the individual Christian and of the whole community, which while being adapted to the conditions of the present time, should nevertheless witness to the evangelical spirit of penance and also be to the advantage of others.

The role of the church in penitential practices is not to be neglected and encouragement given to pray for sinners, and this intention should be included in the prayer of the faithful.[17]

15. "The faithful are to be encouraged to participate in an ever more intense and fruitful way in the Lenten liturgy and in penitential celebrations. They are to be clearly reminded that both according to the law and tradition they should approach the sacrament of penance during this season so that with purified hearts they may participate in the paschal mysteries. It is appropriate that during Lent the sacrament of penance be celebrated according to the rite for the reconciliation of several penitents with individual confession and absolution, as given in the Roman Ritual."[18]

Pastors should devote themselves to the ministry of reconciliation and provide sufficient time for the faithful to avail themselves of this sacrament.

16. "All Lenten observances should be of such a nature that they also witness to the life of the local church and foster it. The Roman tradition of the 'stational' churches can be recommended as a model for gathering the faithful in one place. In this way the

faithful can assemble in larger numbers, especially under the leadership of the bishop of the diocese, or at the tombs of the saints, or in the principal churches of the city or sanctuaries, or some place of pilgrimage which has a special significance for the diocese."[19]

17. "In Lent the altar should not be decorated with flowers, and musical instruments may be played only to give necessary support to the singing";[20] this is in order that the penitential character of the season be preserved.

18. Likewise, from the beginning of Lent until the Paschal Vigil, Alleluia is to be omitted in all celebrations, even on solemnities and feasts.[21]

19. The chants to be sung in celebrations especially of the eucharist and also at devotional exercises should be in harmony with the spirit of the season and the liturgical texts.

20. Devotional exercises which harmonize with the Lenten season are to be encouraged, for example, the Stations of the Cross; they should help foster the liturgical spirit with which the faithful can prepare themselves for the celebration of Christ's paschal mystery.

c) Particular Details Concerning the Days of Lent

21. "On the Wednesday before the first Sunday of Lent, the faithful receive ashes, thus entering into the time established for the purification of their souls. This sign of penance, a traditionally biblical one, has been preserved among the church's customs until the present day. It signifies the human condition of the sinner, who seeks to express his guilt before the Lord in an exterior manner and by so doing expresses his interior conversion, led on by the confident hope that the Lord will be merciful. This same sign marks the beginning of the way of conversion, which is developed through the celebration of the sacraments of penance during the days before Easter."[22]

The blessing and imposition of ashes should take place either in the Mass or outside of the Mass. In the latter case it is to be part of a Liturgy of the Word and conclude with the prayer of the faithful.[23]

22. Ash Wednesday is to be observed as a day of penance in the whole church, one of both abstinence and fasting.[24]

23. The first Sunday of Lent marks the beginning of the annual Lenten observance.[25] In the Mass of this Sunday there should be some distinctive elements which underline this important moment; e.g., the entrance procession with litanies of the saints.[26] During the Mass of the first Sunday in Lent, the bishop should celebrate the rite of election in the cathedral or in some other church as seems appropriate.[27]

24. The Gospel pericopes of the Samaritan woman, of the man blind from birth and the resurrection of Lazarus are assigned to the third, fourth and fifth Sundays of Lent of Year A; of particular significance in relation to Christian initiation, they can also be read in Years B and C, especially in places where there are catechumens.[28]

25. On the fourth Sunday of Lent (Laetare) and on solemnities and feasts, musical instruments may be played and the altar decorated with flowers. Rose-colored vestments may be worn on this Sunday.[29]

26. The practice of covering the crosses and images in the church may be observed if the episcopal conference should so decide. The crosses are to be covered until the end of the celebration of the Lord's Passion on Good Friday. Images are to remain covered until the beginning of the Easter Vigil.[30]

II. Holy Week

27. During Holy Week the church celebrates the mysteries of salvation accomplished by Christ in the last days of his life on earth, beginning with his messianic entrance into Jerusalem.

The Lenten season lasts until the Thursday of this week. The Easter triduum begins with the evening Mass of the Lord's Supper, is continued through Good Friday with the celebration of the Passion of the Lord and Holy Saturday, to reach its summit in the Easter Vigil and concludes with Vespers of Easter Sunday.

"The days of Holy Week, from Monday to Thursday inclusive, have precedence over all other celebrations."[31] It is not fitting that baptisms and confirmations be celebrated on these days.

a) Passion Sunday (Palm Sunday)

28. Holy Week begins on Passion (or Palm) Sunday, which joins the foretelling of Christ's regal triumph and the proclama-

tion of the Passion. The connection between both aspects of the paschal mystery should be shown and explained in the celebration and catechesis of this day.[32]

29. The commemoration of the entrance of the Lord into Jerusalem has according to ancient custom been celebrated with a solemn procession in which the faithful in song and gesture imitate the Hebrew children who went to meet the Lord singing hosanna.[33]

The procession may take place only once before the Mass which has the largest attendance, even if this should be in the evening either of Saturday or Sunday. The congregation should assemble in a secondary church or chapel or in some other suitable place distinct from the church to which the procession will move.

In this procession the faithful carry palm or other branches. The priest and the ministers, also carrying branches, precede the people.[34]

The palms or branches are blessed so that they can be carried in the procession. The palms should be taken home, where they will serve as a reminder of the victory of Christ which they celebrated in the procession.

Pastors should make every effort to ensure that this procession in honor of Christ, the king, be so prepared and celebrated that it is of great spiritual significance in the life of the faithful.

30. The missal, in order to commemorate the entrance of the Lord into Jerusalem, in addition to the solemn procession described above, gives two other forms, not simply for convenience, but to provide for those situations when it will not be possible to have the procession.

The second form is that of a solemn entrance, when the procession cannot take place outside the church. The third form is a simple entrance such as is used at all Masses on this Sunday which do not have the solemn entrance.[35]

31. Where the Mass cannot be celebrated, there should be a celebration of the word of God on the theme of the Lord's messianic entrance and passion, either on Saturday evening or on Sunday at a convenient time.[36]

32. During the procession, the choir and people should sing the chants proposed in the Roman Missal, especially Psalms 23 and 46, as well as other appropriate songs in honor of Christ, the king.

33. The Passion narrative occupies a special place. It should be sung or read in the traditional way, that is, by three persons who take the part of Christ, the narrator and the people. The Passion is proclaimed by deacons or priests, or by lay readers; in the latter case, the part of Christ should be reserved to the priest.

The proclamation of the Passion should be without candles and incense, the greeting and the signs of the cross are omitted; only a deacon asks for the blessing, as he does before the Gospel.[37]

For the spiritual good of the faithful the Passion should be proclaimed in its entirety, and the readings which precede it should not be omitted.

34. After the Passion has been proclaimed, a homily is to be given.

b) The Chrism Mass

35. The Chrism Mass, which the bishop concelebrates with his presbyterium and at which the holy chrism is consecrated and the oils blessed, manifests the communion of the priests with their bishop in the same priesthood and ministry of Christ.[38] At this Mass the priests who concelebrate with the bishop should come from different parts of the diocese, thus showing in the consecration of the chrism to be his witnesses and cooperators just as in their daily ministry they are his helpers and counselors.

The faithful are also to be encouraged to participate in this Mass and to receive the sacrament of the eucharist.

Traditionally the Chrism Mass is celebrated on the Thursday of Holy Week. If, however, it should prove difficult for the clergy and people to gather with the bishop, this rite can be transferred to another day, but one always close to Easter.[39] The chrism and the oil of catechumens is to be used in the celebration of the sacraments of initiation on Easter night.

36. There should be only one celebration of the Chrism Mass, given its significance in the life of the diocese, and it should take place in the cathedral or, for pastoral reasons, in another church[40] which has a special significance.

The holy oils can be brought to the individual parishes before the celebration of the evening Mass of the Lord's Supper or at some other suitable time. This can be a means of catechizing the faithful about the use and effects of the holy oils and chrism in Christian life.

c) The Penitential Celebrations in Lent

37. It is fitting that the Lenten season should be concluded, both for the individual Christian as well as for the whole Christian community, with a penitential celebration, so that they may be helped to prepare to celebrate more fully the paschal mystery.[41]

These celebrations, however, should take place before the Easter triduum and should not immediately precede the evening Mass of the Lord's Supper.

III. The Easter Triduum in General

38. The greatest mysteries of the redemption are celebrated yearly by the church, beginning with the evening Mass of the Lord's Supper on Holy Thursday until Vespers of Easter Sunday. This time is called "the triduum of the crucified, buried and risen";[42] it is also called the "Easter triduum" because during it is celebrated the paschal mystery, that is, the passing of the Lord from this world to his Father. The church, by the celebration of this mystery, through liturgical signs and sacramentals, is united to Christ, her spouse, in intimate communion.

39. The Easter fast is sacred on the first two days of the triduum, in which according to ancient tradition the church fasts "because the Spouse has been taken away."[43] Good Friday is a day of fasting and abstinence; it is also recommended that Holy Saturday be so observed so that the church, with uplifted and welcoming heart, be ready to celebrate the joys of the Sunday of the resurrection.[44]

40. It is recommended that there be a communal celebration of the office of readings and morning prayer on Good Friday and Holy Saturday. It is fitting that the bishop should celebrate the office in the cathedral, with as far as possible the participation of the clergy and people.[45]

This office, formerly called "Tenebrae," held a special place in the devotion of the faithful as they meditated upon the passion, death and burial of the Lord while awaiting the announcement of the resurrection.

41. For the celebration of the Easter triduum it is necessary that there should be a sufficient number of ministers and assistants, who should be prepared so that they know what their role is in the celebration. Pastors must ensure that the meaning of each part of the celebration be explained to the faithful so that they may participate more fully and fruitfully.

42. The chants of the people and also of the ministers and the celebrating priest are of special importance in the celebration of Holy Week and particularly of the Easter triduum because they add to the solemnity of these days and also because the texts are more effective when sung.

The episcopal conferences are asked, unless provision has already been made, to provide music for those parts which it can be said should always be sung, namely:

a) The general intercessions of Good Friday; the deacon's invitation and the acclamation of the people.

b) Chants for the showing and veneration of the cross.

c) The acclamations during the procession with the paschal candle and the Easter proclamation, the responsorial Alleluia, the litany of the saints and the acclamation after the blessing of water.

Since the purpose of sung texts is also to facilitate the participation of the faithful, they should not be lightly omitted; such texts should be set to music. If the text for use in the liturgy has not yet been set to music, it is possible as a temporary measure to select other similar texts which are set to music. It is, however, fitting that there should be a collection of texts set to music for these celebrations, paying attention to:

a) Chants for the procession and blessing of palms, and for the entrance into church.

b) Chants to accompany the procession with the holy oils.

c) Chants to accompany the procession with the gifts on Holy Thursday in the evening Mass of the Lord's Supper, and hymns to accompany the procession of the blessed sacrament to the place of repose.

d) The responsorial psalms at the Easter Vigil, and chants to accompany the sprinkling with blessed water.

Music should be provided for the Passion narrative, the Easter proclamation and the blessing of baptismal water; obviously the melodies should be of a simple nature in order to facilitate their use.

In larger churches where the resources permit, a more ample use should be made of the church's musical heritage, both ancient and modern, always ensuring that this does not impede the active participation of the faithful.

43. It is fitting that small religious communities, both clerical and lay, and other lay groups should participate in the celebration of the Easter triduum in neighboring principal churches.[46]

Similarly, where the number of participants and ministers is so small that the celebrations of the Easter triduum cannot be carried out with the requisite solemnity, such groups of the faithful should assemble in a larger church.

Also, where there are small parishes with only one priest it is recommended that such parishes should assemble, as far as possible, in a principal church and there participate in the celebrations.

On account of the needs of the faithful, where a pastor has the responsibility for two or more parishes in which the faithful assemble in large numbers and where the celebrations can be carried out with the requisite care and solemnity, the celebrations of the Easter triduum may be repeated in accord with the given norms.[47]

So that seminary students "might live fully Christ's paschal mystery and thus be able to teach those who will be committed to their care,"[48] they should be given a thorough and comprehensive liturgical formulation. It is important during their formative years in the seminary that they should experience fruitfully the solemn Easter celebrations, especially those over which the bishop presides.[49]

IV. Holy Thursday Evening Mass of the Lord's Supper

44. With the celebration of Mass on the evening of Holy Thursday "the church begins the Easter triduum and recalls the Last Supper, in which the Lord Jesus, on the night he was betrayed, showing his love for those who were his own in the world, gave his body and blood under the species of bread and wine, offering to his Father and giving them to the apostles so that they might

partake of them, and he commanded them and their successors in the priesthood to perpetuate this offering."[50]

45. Careful attention should be given to the mysteries which are commemorated in this Mass: the institution of the eucharist, the institution of the priesthood and Christ's command of brotherly love. The homily should explain these points.

46. The Mass of the Lord's Supper is celebrated in the evening, at a time that is more convenient for the full participation of the whole local community. All priests may concelebrate even if on this day they have already concelebrated the Chrism Mass or if, for the good of the faithful, they must celebrate another Mass.[51]

47. Where pastoral considerations require it, the local ordinary may permit another Mass to be celebrated in churches and oratories in the evening, and in the case of true necessity, even in the morning, but only for those faithful who cannot otherwise participate in the evening Mass. Care should nevertheless be taken to ensure that celebrations of this kind do not take place for the benefit of private persons or of small groups and that they are not to the detriment of the main Mass.

According to the ancient tradition of the church, all Masses without the participation of the people are on this day forbidden.[52]

48. The tabernacle should be completely empty before the celebration.[53] Hosts for the communion of the faithful should be consecrated during that celebration.[54] A sufficient amount of bread should be consecrated to provide also for communion on the following day.

49. For the reservation of the blessed sacrament, a place should be prepared and adorned in such a way as to be conducive to prayer and meditation; that sobriety appropriate to the liturgy of these days is enjoined, to the avoidance or suppression of all abuses.[55]

When the tabernacle is located in a chapel separated from the central part of the church, it is appropriate to prepare there the place of repose and adoration.

50. During the singing of the hymn "Gloria in Excelsis," in accordance with local custom the bells may be rung and should thereafter remain silent until the "Gloria in Excelsis" of the Easter Vigil, unless the conference of bishops or the local ordinary for a suitable reason has decided otherwise.[56] During this same period

the organ and other musical instruments may be used only for the purpose of supporting the singing.[57]

51. The washing of the feet of the chosen men which, according to tradition, is performed on this day, represents the service and charity of Christ, who came "not to be served, but to serve."[58] This tradition should be maintained, and its proper significance explained.

52. Gifts for the poor, especially those collected during Lent as the fruit of penance, may be presented in the offertory procession while the people sing "Ubi Caritas Est Vera."[59]

53. It is more appropriate that the eucharist be borne directly from the altar by the deacons or acolytes or extraordinary ministers at the moment of communion for the sick and infirm who must communicate at home, so that in this way they may be more closely united to the celebrating church.

54. After the postcommunion prayer, the procession forms, with the crossbearer at its head. The blessed sacrament, accompanied by lighted candles and incense, is carried through the church to the place of reservation, to the singing of the hymn "Pange Lingua" or some other eucharistic song.[60] This rite of transfer of the blessed sacrament may not be carried out if the liturgy of the Lord's Passion will not be celebrated in that same church on the following day.[61]

55. The blessed sacrament should be reserved in a closed tabernacle or pyx. Under no circumstances may it be exposed in a monstrance.

The place where the tabernacle or pyx is situated must not be made to resemble a tomb, and the expression *tomb* is to be avoided for the chapel of repose is not prepared so as to represent the "Lord's burial" but for the custody of the eucharistic bread that will be distributed in communion on Good Friday.

56. The faithful should be encouraged after the Mass of the Lord's Supper to spend a suitable period of tine during the night in the church in adoration before the blssed sacrament that has been solemnly reserved. Where appropriate, this prolonged eucharistic adoration may be accompanied by the reading of some part of the Gospel of St. John (Chaps. 13–17).

From midnight onward, however, the adoration should be made without external solemnity, for the day of the Lord's Passion has begun.[62]

57. After Mass the altar should be stripped. It is fitting that any crosses in the church be covered with a red or purple veil, unless they have already been veiled on the Saturday before the fifth Sunday of Lent. Lamps should not be lit before the images of saints.

V. Good Friday

58. On this day, when "Christ, our passover was sacrificed,"[63] the church meditates on the Passion of her Lord and Spouse, adores the cross, commemorates her origin from the side of Christ asleep on the cross and intercedes for the salvation of the whole world.

59. On this day, in accordance with ancient tradition, the church does not celebrate the eucharist. Holy communion is distributed to the faithful during the celebration of the Lord's Passion alone, though it may be brought at any time of the day to the sick who cannot take part in the celebration.[64]

60. Good Friday is a day of penance to be observed as of obligation in the whole church, and indeed through abstinence and fasting.[65]

61. All celebration of the sacrament on this day is strictly prohibited, except for the sacraments of penance and anointing of the sick.[66] Funerals are to be celebrated without singing, music or the tolling of bells.

62. It is recommended that on this day the office of readings and morning prayer be celebrated with the participation of the people in the churches (cfr. No. 40).

63. The celebration of the Lord's Passion is to take place in the afternoon, at about 3 o'clock. The time will be chosen as shall seem most appropriate for pastoral reasons in order to allow the people to assemble more easily, for example, shortly after midday or in the late evening, however, not later than 9 o'clock.[67]

64. The order for the celebration of the Lord's Passion (the Liturgy of the Word, the adoration of the cross and holy communion), that stems from an ancient tradition of the church, should be observed faithfully and religiously, and may not be changed by anyone on his own initiative.

65. The priests and ministers proceed to the altar in silence and without any singing. If any words of introduction are to be said, they should be pronounced before the ministers enter.

The priest and ministers make a reverence to the altar, prostrating themselves. This act of prostration, which is proper to the rite of the day, should be strictly observed for it signifies both the abasement of "earthly man,"[68] and also the grief and sorrow of the church.

The faithful, for their part, as the ministers enter should be standing and thereafter should kneel in silent prayer.

66. The readings are to be read in their entirety. The responsorial psalm and the chant before the Gospel are to be sung in the usual manner. The narrative of the Lord's Passion according to John is sung or read in the way prescribed for the previous Sunday (cf. No. 33). After the reading of the Passion, a homily should be given, at the end of which the faithful may be invited to spend a short time in meditation.[69]

67. The general intercessions are to follow the wording and form handed down by ancient tradition, maintaining the full range of intentions so as to signify clearly the universal effect of the Passion of Christ, who hung on the cross for the salvation of the whole world. In case of grave public necessity the local ordinary may permit or prescribe the adding of special intentions.[70]

In this event it is permitted to the priest to select from the prayers of the missal those more appropriate to local circumstances in such a way, however, that the series follows the rule for general intercessions.[71]

68. For veneration of the cross let a cross be used that is of appropriate size and beauty, and let one or other of the forms for this rite as found in the Roman Missal be followed. The rite should be carried out with the splendor worthy of the mystery of our salvation. Both the invitation pronounced at the unveiling of the cross and the people's response should be made in song, and a period of respectful silence is to be observed after each act of veneration, and celebrant standing and holding the raised cross.

69. The cross is to be presented to each of the faithful individually for their adoration, since the personal adoration of the cross is a most important feature in this celebration, and only when necessitated by large numbers of faithful present should the rite of veneration be made simultaneously by all present.[72]

Only one cross should be used for the veneration, as this contributes to the full symbolism of the rite. During the veneration of the cross, the antiphons, "reproaches," and hymns should be sung, so that the history of salvation be commemorated through song.[73] Other appropriate songs may also be sung (cf. No. 42).

70. The priest sings the invitation to the Lord's Prayer, which is then sung by all. The sign of peace is not exchanged. The communion rite is as described in the missal.

During the distribution of communion, Psalm 21 or another suitable song may be sung. When communion has been distributed, the pyx is taken to a place prepared for it outside of the church.

71. After the celebration the altar is stripped, the cross remaining, however, with four candles. An appropriate place (for example, the chapel of respose used for reservation of the eucharist on Maunday Thursday) can be prepared within the church, and there the Lord's cross is placed so that the faithful may venerate and kiss it, and spend some time in meditation.

72. Devotions, such as the Way of the Cross, processions of the Passion and commemorations of the sorrows of the Blessed Virgin Mary are not, for pastoral reasons, to be neglected. The texts and songs used, however, should be adapted to the spirit of the liturgy of this day. Such devotions should be assigned to the time of day that makes it quite clear that the liturgical celebration by its very nature far surpasses them in importance.[74]

VI. Holy Saturday

73. On Holy Saturday the church is as it were at the Lord's tomb, meditating on his passion and death, and on his descent into hell,[75] and awaiting his resurrection with prayer and fasting. It is highly recommended that on this day the office of readings and morning prayer be celebrated with the participation of the people (cf. No. 40).[76] Where this cannot be done, there should be some celebration of the word of God or some act of devotion suited to the mystery celebrated this day.

74. The image of Christ crucified or lying in the tomb, or descent into hell, which mystery Holy Saturday recalls, as also an image of the sorrowful Virgin Mary, can be placed in the church for the veneration of the faithful.

75. On this day the church abstains strictly from celebration of the sacrifice of the Mass.[77] Holy communion may only be given in the form of viaticum. The celebration of marriages is forbidden

as also the celebration of other sacraments, except those of penance and the anointing of the sick.

76. The faithful are to be instructed on the special character of Holy Saturday.[78] Festive customs and traditions associated with this day on account of the former practice of anticipating the Easter celebration on Holy Saturday should be reserved for Easter night and the day that follows.

VII. Easter Sunday of the Lord's Resurrection

a) The Easter Vigil

77. According to a most ancient tradition, this night is "one of vigil for the Lord,"[79] and the vigil is celebrated during it to commemorate that holy night when the Lord rose from the dead is regarded as the "mother of all holy vigils."[80] For in that night the church keeps vigil, waiting for the resurrection of the Lord, and celebrates the sacraments of Christian initiation.[81]

1. The Meaning of the Nocturnal Character of the Easter Vigil

78. "The entire celebration of the Easter Vigil takes place at night. It should not begin before nightfall; it should end before daybreak on Sunday."[82] This rule is to be taken according to its strictest sense. Reprehensible are those abuses and practices which have crept in many places in violation of this ruling, whereby the Easter Vigil is celebrated at the time of day that it is customary to celebrate anticipated Sunday Masses.[83]

Those reasons which have been advanced in some quarters for the anticipation of the Easter Vigil such as lack of public order, are not put forward in connection with Christmas night nor other gatherings of various kinds.

79. The Passover vigil, in which the Hebrews kept watch for the Lord's Passover, which was to free them from slavery to pharaoh, is an annual commemoration. It prefigured the true Pasch of Christ that was to come, the night that is of true liberation, in which "destroying the bonds of death, Christ rose as victor from the depths."[84]

80. From the very outset the church has celebrated that annual Pasch, which is the solemnity of solemnities, above all by means of a night vigil. For the resurrection of Christ is the foundation of

our faith and hope, and through baptism and confirmation we are inserted into the paschal mystery of Christ, dying, buried and raised with him, and with him we shall also reign.[85]

The full meaning of vigil is a waiting for the coming of the Lord.[86]

2. The Structure of the Easter Vigil and the Significance of Its Different Elements and Parts

81. The order for the Easter Vigil is so arranged so that after the service of light and the Easter proclamation (which is the first part of the vigil), holy church meditates on the wonderful works which the Lord God wrought for his people from the earliest times (the second part or Liturgy of the Word) to the moment when, together with those new members reborn in baptism (third part), she is called to the table prepared by the Lord for his church, the commemoration of his death and resurrection, until he comes (fourth part).[87]

This liturgical order must not be changed by anyone on his own initiative.

82. The first part consists of symbolic acts and gestures which require that they be performed in all their fullness and nobility so that their meaning, as explained by the introductory words of the celebrant and the liturgical prayer, may be truly understood by the faithful.

Insofar as possible, a suitable place should be prepared outside the church for the blessing of the new fire, whose flames should be such that they genuinely dispel the darkness and light up the night.

The paschal candle should be prepared, which for effecive symbolism must be made of wax, never be artificial, be renewed each year, be only one in number and be of sufficiently large size so that it may evoke the truth that Christ is the light of the world. It is blessed with the signs and words prescribed in the missal or by the conference of bishops.[88]

83. The procession by which the people enter the church should be led by the light of the paschal candle alone. Just as the children of Israel were guided at night by a pillar of fire, so similarly Christians follow the risen Christ. There is no reason why to each response "Thanks be to God" there should not be added some acclamation in honor of Christ.

The light from the paschal candle should be gradually passed to the candles which it is fitting that all present should hold in their hands, the electric lighting being switched off.

84. The deacon makes the Easter proclamation, which tells by means of a great poetic text the whole Easter mystery placed in the context of the economy of salvation. In case of necessity, where there is no deacon and the celebrating priest is unable to sing it, a cantor may do so. The bishops conferences may adapt this proclamation by inserting into it acclamations from the people.[89]

85. The readings from Sacred Scripture constitute the second part of the vigil. They give an account of the outstanding deeds of the history of salvation, which the faithful are helped to meditate calmly upon by the singing of the responsorial psalm, by a silent pause and by the celebrant's prayer.

The restored order for the vigil has seven readings from the Old Testament, chosen from the law and the prophets, which are everywhere in use according to the most ancient tradition of East and West, and two readings from the New Testament, namely from the apostle and from the Gospel. Thus the church, "beginning with Moses and all the prophets," explains Christ's paschal mystery.[90] Consequently, wherever this is possible all the readings should be read in order that the character of the Easter Vigil, which demands that it be somewhat prolonged, be respected at all costs.

Where, however, pastoral conditions require that the number of readings be reduced, there should be at least three readings from the Old Testament, taken from the law and the prophets, and the reading from Exodus 14 with its canticle must never be omitted.[91]

86. The typological import of the Old Testament texts is rooted in the New and is made plain by the prayer pronounced by the celebrating priest after each reading; but it will also be helpful to introduce the people to the meaning of each reading by means of a brief introduction. This introduction may be given by the priest himself or by a deacon.

National or diocesan liturgical commissions will prepare aids for pastors.

Each reading is followed by the singing of a psalm, to which the people respond.

Melodies should be provided for these responses, which are capable of promoting the people's participation and devotion.[92] Great care is to be taken that trivial songs do not take the place of the psalms.

87. After the readings from the Old Testament, the hymn "Gloria in Excelsis," the bells are rung in accordance with local custom, the collect is recited and the celebration moves on to the readings from the New Testament. There is read an exhortation from the apostle on baptism as an insertion into Christ's paschal mystery.

Then all stand, and the priest intones the Alleluia three times, each time raising the pitch. The people repeat it after him.[93] If it is necessary, the psalmist or cantor may sing the Alleluia, which the people then take up as an acclamation to be interspersed between the verses of Psalm 117, which is so often cited by the apostles in their Easter preaching.[94] Finally the resurrection of the Lord is proclaimed from the Gospel as the high point of the whole Liturgy of the Word. After the Gospel a homily is to be given, no matter how brief.

88. The third part of the vigil is the baptismal liturgy. Christ's passover and ours is now celebrated. This is given full expression in those churches which have a baptismal font and more so when the Christian initiation of adults is held or at least the baptism of infants.[95] Even if there are no candidates for baptism, the blessing of baptismal water should still take place in parish churches. If this blessing does not take place at the baptismal font but in the sanctuary, baptismal water should be carried afterward to the baptistery, there to be kept throughout the whole of paschal time.[96] Where there are neither candidates for baptism nor any need to bless the font, baptism should be commemorated by a blessing of water destined for sprinkling upon the people.[97]

89. Next follows the renewal of baptismal promises, introduced by some words on the part of the celebrating priest. The faithful reply to the questions put to them, standing and holding lighted candles in their hand. They are then sprinkled with water; in this way the gestures and words recall to them the baptism they have received. The celebrating priest sprinkles the people by passing through the main part of the church while all sing the antiphon "Vidi Aquam" or another suitable song of a baptismal character.[98]

90. The celebration of the eucharist forms the fourth part of the vigil and marks its high point, for it is in the fullest sense the Easter sacrament, that is to say, the commemoration of the sacrifice of the cross and the presence of the risen Christ, the completion of Christian initiation and the foretaste of the eternal Pasch.

91. Great care should be taken that this eucharistic liturgy is not celebrated in haste; indeed, all the rites and words must be given their full force: the general intercessions in which for the first time the neophytes now as members of the faithful exercise their priesthood;[99] the procession at the offertory in which the neophytes, if there are any, take part; the first, second or third eucharistic prayer, preferably sung, with their proper embolisms;[100] and finally eucharistic communion, as the moment of full participation in the mystery that is being celebrated. It is appropriate that at communion there be sung Psalm 117 with the antiphon "Pascha Nostrum" or Psalm 33 with the antiphon "Alleluia, Alleluia, Alleluia" or some other song of Easter exultation.

92. It is fitting that in the communion of the Easter Vigil full expression be given to the symbolism of the eucharist, namely by consuming the eucharist under the species of both bread and wine. The local ordinaries will consider the appropriateness of such a concession and its ramifications.[101]

3. Some Pastoral Considerations

93. The Easter Vigil liturgy should be celebrated in such a way as to offer to the Christian people the riches of the prayers and rites. It is therefore important that authenticity be respected, that the participation of the faithful be promoted and that the celebration should not take place without servers, readers and choir exercising their role.

94. It would be desirable if on occasion provision were made for several communities to assemble in one church wherever their proximity one to another or small numbers mean that a full and festive celebration could not otherwise take place.

The celebration of the Easter Vigil for special groups is not to be encouraged, since above all in this vigil the faithful should come together as one and should experience a sense of ecclesial community.

The faithful who are absent from their parish on vacation should be urged to participate in the liturgical celebration in the place where they happen to be.

95. In announcements concerning the Easter Vigil care should be taken not to present it as the concluding period of Holy Saturday, but rather it should be stressed that the Easter Vigil is celebrated "during Easter night," and that it is one single act of worship. Pastors should be advised that in giving catechesis to the people they should be taught to participate in the vigil in its entirety.[102]

96. For a better celebration of the Easter Vigil, it is necessary that pastors themselves have an ever deeper knowledge of both text and rites so as to give a proper mystagogical catechesis to the people.

b) *Easter Day*

97. Mass is to be celebrated on Easter Day with great solemnity. It is appropriate that the penitential rite on this day take the form of a sprinkling with water blessed at the vigil, during which the antiphon "Vidi Aquam" or some other song of baptismal character should be sung. The fonts at the entrance to the church should also be filled with the same water.

98. The tradition of celebrating baptismal Vespers on Easter Day with the singing of psalms during the procession to the font should be maintained where it is still in force, and as appropriate restored.[103]

99. The paschal candle has its proper place either by the ambo or by the altar and should be lit at least in all the more solemn liturgical celebrations of the season until Pentecost Sunday, whether at Mass or at morning and evening prayer. After the Easter season the candle should be kept with honor in the baptistery, so that in the celebration of baptism the candles of the baptized may be lit from them. In the celebration of funerals the paschal candle should be placed near the coffin to indicate that the death of a Christian is his own passover. The paschal candle should not otherwise be lit nor placed in the sanctuary outside the Easter season.[104]

VIII. Easter Time

100. The celebration of Easter is prolonged throughout the Easter season. The 50 days from Easter Sunday to Pentecost Sunday are celebrated as one feast day, the "great Sunday."[105]

101. The Sundays of this season are regarded as Sundays of Easter and so termed, and they have precedence over all feasts of the Lord and over all solemnities. Solemnities that fall on one of these Sundays are anticipated on the Saturday.[106] Celebrations in honor of the Blessed Virgin Mary or the saints which fall during the week may not be transferred to one of these Sundays.[107]

102. For adults who have received Christian initiation during the Easter Vigil the whole of this period is given over to mystagogical catechesis. Therefore wherever there are neophytes the prescriptions of the Rite of Christian Initiation of Adults, Nos. 37–40 and 235–239, should be observed. Intercession should be made in the eucharistic prayer for the newly baptized through the Easter octave in all places.

103. Throughout the Easter season the neophytes should be assigned their own special place among the faithful. All neophytes should endeavor to participate at Mass along with their godparents. In the homily and, according to local circumstances, in the general intercessions mention should be made of them. Some celebration should be held to conclude the period of mystagogical catechesis on or about Pentecost Sunday, depending upon local custom.[108] It is also appropriate that children receive their first communion on one or other of the Sundays of Easter.

104. During Easter time, pastors should instruct the faithful who have been already initiated into the eucharist on the meaning of the church's precept concerning the reception of holy communion during this period.[109] It is also highly recommended that communion be brought to the sick also, especially during the Easter octave.

105. Where there is the custom of blessing houses in celebration of the resurrection, this blessing is to be imparted after the solemnity of Easter, and not before, by the parish priest or other priests or deacons delegated by him. This is an opportunity for exercising a pastoral ministry.[110] The parish priest should go to each

house for the purpose of undertaking a pastoral visitation of each family. There he will speak with the residents, spend a few moments with them in prayer using texts to be found in the Book of Blessings.[111] In larger cities consideration should be given to the gathering of several families for a common celebration of the blessing for all.

106. According to the differing circumstances of places and peoples, there are found a number of popular practices linked to celebrations of the Easter season, which in some instances attract greater numbers of the people than the sacred liturgy itself; these are not in any way to be undervalued, for they are often well adapted to the religious mentality of the faithful. Let episcopal conferences and local ordinaries, therefore, see to it that practices of this kind, which seem to nourish popular piety, be harmonized in the best way possible with the sacred liturgy, be imbued more distinctly with the spirit of the liturgy, in some way derived from it, and lead the people to it.[112]

107. This sacred period of 50 days concludes with Pentecost Sunday, when the gift of the Holy Spirit to the apostles, the beginnings of the church and the start of its mission to all tongues and peoples and nations are commemorated.[113]

Encouragement should be given to the prolonged celebration of Mass in the form of a vigil whose character is not baptismal as in the Easter Vigil, but is one of urgent prayer, after the example of the apostles and disciples, who persevered together in prayer with Mary, the mother of Jesus, as they awaited the Holy Spirit.[114]

108. "It is proper to the paschal festivity that the whole church rejoices at the forgiveness of sins, which is not only for those who are reborn in holy baptism, but also for those who have long been numbered among the adopted children."[115] By means of a more intensive pastoral care and a deeper spiritual effort, all who celebrate the Easter feasts will by the Lord's grace experience their effect in their daily lives.[116]

Given at Rome, at the offices of the Congregation for Divine Worship, Jan. 16, 1988.

Cardinal Paul Augustine Mayer
Prefect

Archbishop Virgilio Noe
Secretary

Footnotes

1. Cf. Congregation for Rites, decree *Dominicae Resurrectionis* (Feb. 9, 1951) AAS 43 (1951) 128–137; ibid., decree *Maxima Redemptionis Nostrae Mysteria* (Nov. 16, 1955) AAS 47 (1955) 838–847.

2. Cf. Second Vatican Council, Constitution on the Sacred Liturgy, 5, 6, 61.

3. Cf. General Norms for the Liturgical Year and the Calendar, 18.

4. Cf. Second Vatican Council, Decree on the Pastoral Office of Bishops, 15.

5. Cf. *Maxima Redemptionis Nostrae Mysteria.*

6. Cf. Ceremonial of Bishops, 249.

7. Cf. The Roman Ritual, Rite of Christian Initiation of Adults, 8; Code of Canon Law, Canon 856.

8. Roman Missal, the Easter Vigil, 46.

9. Cf. Rite of Christian Initiation of Adults, Chap. 4, especially No. 303.

10. Cf. ibid., 330–333.

11. Cf. Ceremonial of Bishops, 250, 406–407; cf. Rite of Christian Initiation of Adults, 41.

12. Cf. General Norms for the Liturgical Year and the Calendar, 5; cf. ibid., 56f, and *Notitiae*, 23 (1987) 397.

13. Ibid. 16,b).

14. Roman Missal, General Instruction, 42; cf. Rite of Penance, 36–37.

15. Paul VI, Apostolic Constitution on Penance, 11, 1; AAS 58 (1966) 183.

16. Ceremonial of Bishops, 251.

17. Cf. ibid., 251; Constitution on the Sacred Liturgy, 109.

18. Cf. Ceremonial of Bishops, 251.

19. Cf. ibid., 260.

20. Ibid., 252.

21. Cf. General Norms for the Liturgical Year and Calendar, 28.

22. Cf. Ceremonial for Bishops, 253.

23. Roman Missal, Ash Wednesday.

24. Apostolic Constitution on Penance, 11, 1; Canon 1251.

25. Roman Missal, First Sunday of Lent, opening prayer and prayer over the gifts.

26. Cf. Ceremonial of Bishops, 261.

27. Cf. ibid., 408–410.

28. Roman Missal, Lectionary for Mass, 2nd ed., 1981. Introduction, 97.

29. Cf. Ceremonial of Bishops, 252.

30. Roman Missal, rubric Saturday of the fourth week of Lent.

31. Cf. General Norms for the Liturgical Year and the Calendar, 16, a.

32. Cf. Ceremonial of Bishops, 263.

33. Cf. Roman Missal, Passion Sunday (Palm Sunday), 9.

34. Cf. Ceremonial of Bishops, 270.

35. Cf. Roman Missal, Passion Sunday (Palm Sunday), 16.

36. Cf. ibid., 19.

37. Cf. ibid., 22. For a Mass at which a bishop presides, cf. Ceremonial of Bishops, 74.

38. Second Vatican Council, Decree on the Ministry and Life of Priests, 7.

39. Ceremonial of Bishops, 275.

40. Cf. ibid., 276.

41. Cf. Rite of Penance, Appendix II, 1, 7; cf. above, 18.

42. Cf. *Maxima Redemptionis Nostrae Mysteria*; St. Augustine, Ep. 55, 24, *Patrologia Latina*, 35, 215.

43. Cf. Mk 2:19–20; Tertullien, *De ieiunio* 2 and 13, Collected Works of Christian Writers, Latin series, II, p. 1271.

44. Cf. Ceremonial of Bishops, 295; Constitution on the Sacred Liturgy, 110.

45. Cf. Ibid., 296; General Instruction of the Liturgy of the Hours, 210.

46. Cf. Congregation of Rites, Instruction on the Worship of the Eucharistic Mystery (May 25, 1967), 26: AAS 59 (1967) 558. N.B. In monasteries of nuns, every effort should be made to celebrate the Easter triduum with the greatest possible ceremony but within the monastery church.

47. Cf. Congregation for Rites, *Ordinationes et Declarationes Circa Ordinem Hebdomadae Sanctae Instauratum* (Feb. 1, 1957), 21: AAS 49 (1957) 91–95.

48. Second Vatican Council, Decree on Priestly Formation, 8.

49. Cf. Congregation for Catholic Education, Instruction on Liturgical Formation in Seminaries (May 17, 1979) 15, 33.

50. Cf. Ceremonial of Bishops, 297.

51. Cf. Roman Missal, Evening Mass of the Lord's Supper.

52. Cf. ibid.

53. Cf. ibid., 1.

54. Constitution on the Sacred Liturgy, 55; Instruction on Worship of the Eucharistic Mystery, 31.

55. *Maxima Redemptionis Nostrae Mysteria*, 9.

56. Cf. Roman Missal, Evening Mass of the Lord's Supper.

57. Cf. Ceremonial of Bishops, 300.

58. Mt. 20:28.

59. Cf. Ceremonial of Bishops, 303.

60. Cf. Roman Missal, Evening Mass of the Lord's Supper, 15–16.

61. Cf. Congregation for Rites, Declaration of March 15, 1956, 3: AAS 48 (1956) 153; *Ordinationes et Declarationes Circa Ordinem Hebdomadae Sanctae Instauratum* 14.

62. Cf. Roman Missal, Evening Mass of the Lord's Supper, 21; *Maxima Redemptionis Nostrae Mysteria*, 8–10.

63. 1 Cor. 5:7.

64. Cf. Roman Missal, Good Friday, Celebration of the Lord's Passion, 1, 3.

65. Apostolic Constitution on Penance, II, 2; Canon 1251.

66. Cf. Roman Missal, Good Friday, Celebration of the Lord's Passion, 1; Congregation for Divine Worship, declaration *Ad Missale Romanum*, in Notitiae 13 (1977) 602.

67. Cf. ibid., 3; *Ordinationes et Declarationes Circa Ordinem Hebdomadae Sanctae Instauratum*, 15.

68. Cf. ibid., 5, alternative prayer.

69. Cf. ibid., 9; cf. Ceremonial of Bishops, 319.

70. Cf. ibid., 12.

71. Cf. Roman Missal, General Instruction, 46.

72. Cf. Roman Missal, Good Friday, Celebration of the Lord's Passion, 19.

73. Cf. Mi. 6:3–4.

74. Cf. Constitution on the Sacred Liturgy, 13.

75. Cf. Roman Missal, Holy Saturday; The Apostles' Creed; 1 Pt. 3:19.

76. Cf. General Instruction on the Liturgy of the Hours, 210.

77. Roman Missal, Holy Saturday.

78. *Maxima Redemptionis Nostrae Mysteria*, 2.

79. Cf. Ex. 12:42.

80. St. Augustine, Sermon 219, PL 38, 1088.

81. Ceremonial of Bishops, 332.

82. Cf. ibid.; Roman Missal, The Easter Vigil, 3.

83. Instruction on the Worship of the Eucharistic Mystery, 28.

84. Roman Missal, Easter Vigil, 19, Easter Proclamation.

85. Cf. Constitution on the Sacred Liturgy, 6; cf. Rom. 6:3–6; Eph. 2:5–6; Col. 2:12–13; 2 Tm. 2:11–12.

86. "We keep vigil on that night because the Lord rose from the dead; that life . . . where there is no longer the sleep of death, began for us in his flesh; being thus risen, death will be no more nor have dominion . . . If we have kept vigil for the risen one, he will see that we shall reign with him forever." St. Augustine, *Sermo Guelferbytan.*, 5, 4, PLS 2, 552.

87. Cf. Roman Missal, Easter Vigil, 7.

88. Cf. ibid., 10–12.

89. Cf. ibid., 17.

90. Lk 24:27; cf. Lk 24:44–45.

91. Cf. Roman Missal, Easter Vigil, 21.

92. Cf. ibid., 23.

93. Cf. Ceremonial of Bishops, 352.

94. Cf. Acts 4:11–12; Mt. 21:42; Mk. 12:10; Lk. 20:17.

95. Cf. The Roman Ritual, Rite of Baptism for Children, 6.

96. Cf. Roman Missal, Easter Vigil, 48.

97. Cf. ibid., 45.

98. Cf. ibid., 47.

99. Cf. ibid., 49; Rite of Christian Initiation of Adults, 36.

100. Cf. Roman Missal, Easter Vigil, 53; ibid., Ritual Masses, 3, Baptism.

101. Cf. Roman Missal, General Instruction, 240–242.

102. Cf. Constitution on the Sacred Liturgy, 106.

103. Cf. General Instruction of the Liturgy of the Hours, 213.

104. Cf. Roman Missal, Pentecost Sunday, final rubric; The Roman Ritual, Rite of Baptism for Children, Christian Initiation, General Introduction, 25.

105. Cf. General Norms for the Liturgical Year and the Calendar, 22.

106. Cf. ibid., 5, 23.

107. Cf. ibid., 58.

108. Cf. Rite of Christian Initiation of Adults, 235–237; cf. ibid., 238–239.

109. Cf. Canon 920.

110. *Maxima Redemptionis Nostrae Mysteria*, 24.

111. Book of Blessings, Chaps. 1, 2; Blessing of a Family in Its Own Home.

112. Cf. Constitution on the Sacred Liturgy, 13; cf. Congregation for Divine Worship, *Orientamenti e Proposte per la Celebrazione dell'Anno Mariano*, (April 3, 1987) 3, 51–56.

113. Cf. General Norms for the Liturgical Year and the Calendar, 23.

114. It is possible to combine the celebration of first Vespers with the celebration of Mass as provided for in the General Instruction of the Liturgy of the Hours, 96. In order to throw into greater relief the mystery of this day, it is possible to have several readings from Holy Scripture, as proposed in the Lectionary. In this case, after the collect the reader goes to the ambo to proclaim the reading. The psalmist or cantor sings the psalm, to which the people respond with the refrain. Then all stand and the priest says, "Let us pray," and after a short silent pause he says the prayer corresponding to the reading (for example, one of the collects for the ferial days of the seventh week of Easter).

115. St. Leo the Great, Sermo 6 de Quadragesima, 1–2, PL 54, 285.

116. Cf. Roman Missal, Saturday of the Seventh Week of Easter, Opening Prayer.

Kenneth F. Jenkins

FOUR

LENT'S MULTILAYERED MEANINGS

Of all the liturgical seasons perhaps the most devoutly observed yet least understood is Lent. While some Catholics might confess confusion about which days to fast on or on which to abstain from meat, most would say that Lent involves some sort of forty-day sacrifice. Childhood reflections of "giving up" something for Lent, whether that be candy or fighting with siblings, aren't far from most minds. Yet how often do such fading memories serve as the basis for what most Catholics—at least the "church every Sunday" ones—understand about Lent?

In preparing for this article, I asked a group of adults about their present understanding of Lent. Their responses, though something of a surprise, support just what the circular letter on "Preparing and Celebrating the Paschal Feasts" calls the "inadequate formation given to the clergy and the faithful." This lack of formation, the letter continues, has inhibited the full understanding and, therefore, the full celebration of the "paschal mystery as the center of the liturgical year and of Christian life" (no. 3).

Most of the people I asked agreed that Lent is an important season, but there was little agreement about its possible meaning. One person said that it's a time to enter into the passion and death of Christ, while another said that Lent is about penance in reparation for our sins. A third thought these "dreary weeks," as he called them, were set aside for spiritual reflection and personal improvement. When I asked if there was a relationship between Lent and Easter, I was astounded that this trio of college educated, parochially involved, practicing Catholics saw little relationship between the two seasons other than the fact that one followed the other. It may be understandable that the full impact of the Rite of Christian Initiation of Adults has yet to reach them or even that they do not grasp how the Sunday readings lead to the celebration of the triduum. But not to grasp the basic connection between Lent and Easter suggests a significant lacuna in their knowledge of the basic Christian liturgical tradition.

It is rather difficult to celebrate the depth of the Lenten season, let alone the fullness of Easter joy, if parish churches are filled with faithful Catholics who have yet to move beyond their childhood understandings. This circular letter offers all of us in positions of liturgical leadership a challenge to take stock of how our Lenten celebrations reflect the rich personal and communal meaning of the season and whether these weeks really prepare a community for fifty days of unbounded joy.

It has been said that studying history liberates us from the misconceptions of the present. A brief outline of Lent's historical development, then, may help to set aside misconceptions and make better sense of the multiple strata of meanings that have piled one atop another over the centuries.

LENT'S LAYERS OF MEANING

Lent did not begin as a commemoration of Jesus' journey to Jerusalem. In fact, the days we call "Lent" originally developed as a reflection of Jesus' desert experience in preparation for his public ministry. By the late third or early fourth century C.E. an extended period of fasting was observed in northern Africa as a penitential practice. The length of the fast varied from place to place and year to year; only much later was a length of forty days commonly accepted. Those who took part in the fast were described as being nourished on small amounts of bread and water and on the Scriptures that were read at communal prayer services. Some local churches embraced the penitential nature of the fast more rigorously than others by providing an opportunity to begin, and ultimately conclude, a process of reconciliation for public sinners. As the catechumenate developed, these days of fasting provided an excellent opportunity to incorporate those making their final preparation for sacramental initiation.

The historical formation of Lent did not conclude here, however. As infant baptism took precedence over adult initiation and private confession replaced public "canonical" penance, the thrust of this time of fasting took on a new focus. By the eleventh and twelfth centuries the season came to be viewed principally as a time of personal penance, mortification, prayer, and almsgiving, even though the liturgical texts continued to reflect earlier meanings.

Not until the restoration of the Easter Vigil in the 1950s and the subsequent promulgation of the Constitution on the Sacred Liturgy (CSL, 1963) did the understanding of Lent as a period of final baptismal preparation and spiritual conversion come to fruition. Vatican II described Lent as having a twofold character, being both baptismal and penitential (CSL, no. 109). Moving beyond an inward and personal attitude to penance, the council emphasized the outward and social dimensions of sin, penance, and ultimate reconciliation. With the publication of the interim English translation of the Rite of Christian Initiation of Adults (1974), the Lenten season came to be called "a time for spiritual recollection in preparation for the celebration of the paschal mystery" (RCIA, 1988 U.S. edition, no. 138). At the same time the RCIA described the period of purification and enlightenment for the elect as coinciding with Lent as a time of more intense spiritual preparation. In popular liturgical parlance, Lent has more recently been dubbed a "forty-day retreat" for the elect and the local community as they approach the waters of baptism and the celebration of Easter.

RENEWING THE PROMISES

As we try to cope with all these layers of meaning, what does the circular letter say that is new or that will help us better prepare for Easter? This letter is basically a compilation of norms found in other liturgical documents: it brings together directives found in the sacramentary, the Rite of Christian Initiation of Adults, the General Norms for the Liturgical Year and Calendar, and the Ceremonial of Bishops, the most recently revised and translated component of the Roman Ritual. The letter quotes

from the Ceremonial to describe Lent as having "a double character, namely to prepare both catechumens and faithful to celebrate the paschal mystery" (no. 6; Ceremonial, no. 249). Prayer,
penance, and study for those who are already baptized, in other
words, are to be directed toward a fuller renewal of baptismal
promises as the process of conversion and spiritual development
continues.

Our American individualism tends to provide a somewhat
myoptic view of penance and spiritual development. We are
usually concerned simply with our own personal, individual
development. But just as penance is outward and social, as Vatican II reminded us, so too is the Lenten journey of spiritual
enrichment. The circular letter emphasizes communal gatherings
as opportunities to embrace the Scripture and to expand our
vision of conversion through penance services. Diocesan assem-
blies and processions are also encouraged, although most diocesan and parochial ministers would probably insist that a fine
celebration of the Rite of Election is enough.

The document makes some interesting statements on the nature of the liturgical environment and music. It reminds us that
"the altar should not be decorated with flowers, and musical
instruments may be played only to give necessary support to the
singing" (no. 17). The reason given for such restrictions is to
maintain the penitential character of the season, but it is important to remember that on Sundays, even during Lent, the church
celebrates the fullness of the paschal mystery—the passion,
death, and resurrection of Christ. The victory over sin and death
continues to be proclaimed, and the baptized continue to be
renewed in the eucharist. Sunday is a day of feasting, not fasting,
and even the Lenten season does not regulate the Sunday celebration to one of less joy or thanksgiving.

One can also make a case for the noble simplicity of Lenten
liturgical environments and sensitively orchestrated seasonal
music as hallmarks of American liturgical development. Certainly both should be appropriate reflections of Sunday and Lent,
but ultimately the principal criterion must be whether they encourage the active, conscious participation of the assembly. It is
that participation that leads to a recognition of and response to
God's call to conversion.

Of lesser significance to the document's main point is the confusion that might result from the statement that "the first Sunday of Lent marks the beginning of the annual Lenten observance" (no. 23). The General Norms for the Liturgical Year and the Calendar place Lent's beginning several days earlier, on Ash Wednesday. Both documents calculate the "forty days" of Lent, but each uses a different method. According to the circular letter, Lent begins on the first Sunday, includes all the Sundays of Lent, and concludes as the triduum begins on Holy Thursday. In the General Norms, however, Lent begins on Ash Wednesday, excludes all the Sundays in the period, and runs "until the Mass of the Lord's Supper exclusive" (General Norms, no. 28). Both methods total about forty days. The question that arises is whether these forty days, which were originally days of fasting, should include Sundays and/or the paschal fast that takes place from Good Friday until the Easter Vigil. Such questions should not distract from a better understanding of how Lent can lead to a fuller celebration of Easter.

Final mention should be made of the Sunday readings, particularly the three gospel Sunday readings, particularly the three gospel texts in cycle A in which Jesus gives living water to a Samaritan, restores sight to the blind, and resuscitates a friend to a new hope for life. In each of the Lenten gospel readings, not only in these three that correspond to the Sundays on which the scrutinies are celebrated, images are evoked that will come together at the Easter Vigil and then be developed on the Sundays of the Easter Season. Like a kaleidoscope coming into a brilliant focus, each Lenten turn promises a new addition to a radiant collage as we finally reach the empty tomb.

The full celebration of the Easter feasts necessitates the full observance of Lent. That full observance requires adequate formation first of liturgical ministers and ultimately of all the baptized. Through careful planning of Lent and Easter as two interdependent seasons, quality formation will occur, and that will ultimately lead to the transformation of individuals and communities as together we "climb the holy mountain of Easter" (no. 6).

William J. Freburger

FIVE

PALMS, PASSION, PENANCE, AND OIL

I spent several weeks in July, 1989, living in the village of Corofin in County Clare in the west of Ireland. Corofin's population is five hundred, its main street is a quarter of a mile long, and the parish church, Saint Patrick's, seats three hundred people. The circular letter on "Preparing and Celebrating the Paschal Feasts" was written for Corofin. Its provisions could be implemented there completely without changing a word.

Those of us clustered in our metropolitan areas across the North American continent, however, bring a different perspective to this document. Although the text does not name names, we live in one of those societies whose "certain attitudes ... present difficulties for the faithful to participate in these celebrations" (no. 4). But it is not impossible to celebrate and live the paschal mystery in our American context. American liturgists and pastoral musicians can be thankful for this timely reminder of the mystery's centrality.

Section II of the letter—"Holy Week"—consists of three parts: Passion Sunday (Palm Sunday), the chrism Mass, and penitential celebrations in "Lent" (the head says that, but the text is only concerned with such celebrations during Holy Week).

PALMS AND PASSION

Passion Sunday is the beginning of Holy Week.[1] The text's description of this Sunday points to the first liturgical-catechet-

61

ical-pastoral problem of the day's liturgy. It "joins the foretelling of Christ's regal triumph and the proclamation of the Passion" (no. 28). However, some of the tension inherent in this conjunction of the passion narrative with an anticipation of Easter triumph is diluted by the directive that the full-scale procession ("in honor of Christ the king," no. 29) with palms ("a reminder of the victory of Christ") may take place *only once* in each parish—at the Mass with the largest attendance. Of the other two choices for the entrance rite at Masses this weekend, one is so ritually thin (including neither palms nor people!) as to be laughable as a "commemoration of the Lord's entrance into Jerusalem."

The solemn procession begins in a place "distinct" from the church to which the procession will move" (no. 29), suggesting a procession out of doors. In some years the weather will influence this outdoor procession; in all years, the lack of processional experience will dampen the triumphant experience the letter desires for this opening rite. For the most part, liturgical processions are movements that we *watch*, not ones in which we participate.[2]

Already in the course of Lent, on the Second Sunday, the liturgy assured us that Easter will come. The joyful anticipation of Easter on Passion Sunday is a problem only if it supplies people wth a motive for a "cheap Easter," namely, non-attendance at the triduum celebrations.[3]

The letter mentions music only twice in connection with Passion Sunday: songs to accompany the solemn procession (nos. 29, 32) and singing the passion narrative (no. 33). The passion should be proclaimed in its entirety (even though the lectionary offers an abbreviated version). To alleviate the tedium of length, the letter recommends that the text be sung or read by three persons in the roles of Christ, narrator, and people. Liturgists have objected to such "role-playing," however, because it destroys the sense of one book for proclamation and obscures the gospel's original literary form.

HIJACKED OIL

The second part of the letter's section on Holy Week (II,b,35–36) gathers directives and suggestions for the chrism Mass, traditionally associated with Holy Thursday.[4] Continuing the emphasis on unitary celebration, the text directs that there be only one chrism Mass in each diocese, celebrated on Holy Thursday, if possible. In a bow to the tight schedules of Holy Week (and the holiday period mentioned in no. 4), however, the document allows the transferal of the chrism Mass to another day, "but one always close to Easter" (no. 35). Most dioceses in the United States choose to transfer the Mass to the Monday or Tuesday of Holy Week.

The chrism Mass has two purposes: to consecrate the chrism and bless the oils to be used in the initiation rites at the Easter Vigil and in other sacramental celebrations through the year and to manifest the priesthood shared by bishop, priests, and deacons. Almost as an aside, the text desires that "the faithful . . . be encouraged to participate" (no. 35). They might find such participation discouraging, since the Mass texts are, as British liturgist Christopher Walsh puts it, "unfortunately clericalist, or more specifically sacerdotalist, in tendency.[5] He laments the fact that "this age-old liturgy of oil was more or less hijacked in 1970 by the superimposition of the related but extraneous theme of priesthood for disciplinary and ideological ends particular to the late sixties." The current structure of the chrism Mass certainly seems out of step with the shared pastoral ministry developing in the United States.

The circular letter recommends that the delivery of oils to individual parishes on Holy Thursday be made a teachable moment about their use and effects. But to introduce the oils into the evening Mass is to make them a focus in a celebration in which they play no part. It would make more sense to present them solemnly during the Easter Vigil, at the initiation rites.

FIRING PENITENTIAL BLANKS

The final section of the letter's treatment of Holy Week (II,c,37) urges that the Lenten season be closed "with a penitential celebration" held before the triduum begins, but not immediately before the evening Mass of the Lord's Supper on Holy Thursday. A footnote reveals that the text's author(s) had in mind what we would call a "Bible service," a liturgy of the word with a penitential theme, but with no provision for the sacrament of penance. Indeed the Rite of Penance warns that "care must be taken to ensure that the faithful do not confuse these celebrations with the celebration of the sacrament of penance."[6]

The purpose is to provide some sort of public closure to the season of Lent, but several circumstances militate against this way of doing it. First, aside from the fact that Bible services are a dead letter on the American pastoral scene, a nonsacramental penitential celebration will strike most people as "firing with blanks," especially since communal penance services that include the sacrament have proven so popular over the last twenty years. Second, many parishes schedule communal penance services early in Holy Week, by now a traditional practice that the anemic alternative proposed here would find it hard to preempt. Third, although it would be helpful to signal the end of Lent more strongly than we do, parishes may be reluctant to dilute their Holy Week schedules with yet another celebration to plan, promote, and execute.

Although it is helpful to have gathered in one place, as this letter does, the various liturgical norms regarding Holy Week and the Easter triduum, this text breaks no new ground. Indeed, it does not even offer resolutions of the four "abuses" it cites as the motives for its genesis: the waning of the concept of vigil, the popularity of devotions other than the official celebrations, the inadequate formation of priests and people, and the attitudes of modern society (nos. 3–4). It merely repeats material already on the books.

And it does this in language that is less than inspirational. The translation of the circular letter that accompanies the essays in this volume is the official English translation prepared and distributed by the Vatican. I have decried elsewhere the poor quality of these official English texts,[7] but I will make the point again.

Internal evidence indicates that an American prepared the translation from an Italian and/or Latin original, for the English contains grammatical errors that only and American would make, e.g., "should try *and* attend" (no. 13), "the chrism and the oil . . . *is* to be used" (no. 35), and so on. The translator may have a working knowledge of the languages involved, but the finished product lacks felicity. The passive voice used throughout gives a plodding quality to the text. And at times the English is turgid to the point of meaninglessness. Read the three paragraphs of no. 14 from the section on Lent, and then try to parse them coherently. It is time that we demand official translations of liturgical documents that exhibit the same quality and beauty that we desire for our liturgy.

Notes

1. For a schematic history of the formation of Passion Sunday and Holy Week, see I.H. Dalmais et al., *The Church at Prayer* (new edition), vol. 4, The Liturgy and Time (Collegeville: The Liturgical Press, 1986) 70–72, 75–76; also Adolf Adam, *The Liturgical Year* (New York: Pueblo Publishing Company, 1981) 107–111.

2. See my essay, "A Disturbing Recession in Processions," *The Priest* (June 1986) 20.

3. See my essay, "Restoring the True Character of the Easter Triduum," *The Priest* (April 1989) 27.

4. For a commentary on the chrism Mass, see Adolf Adam, *The Liturgical Year* 112–113.

5. Christopher Walsh, "Indigestion at the Lord's Supper," in *Liturgy*, the review of the Liturgy Office of the Bishops' Conference of England and Wales (February-March 1989) 111–116.

6. Rite of Penance, Introduction, no. 37; see also my essay, "The State of Penance in the Church Today," *The Priest* (October 1986) 30–32.

7. See my remarks in the *National Catholic Reporter*, 13 April 1979, 9; and my essay "Encyclical Translation Disservice to the Church," *The Priest* (April 1987) 28.

David N. Power, O.M.I.

SIX

THE EASTER TRIDUUM CRUCIFIED, BURIED, AND RISEN

The purpose of nos. 38–43 of the document is to stress the unity of the triduum and to make some general suggestions as to its celebration. The document follows the principles adopted in the reforms of Pius XII in 1955 with regard to the triduum's composition: it begins with the commemoration of the Last Supper on Thursday evening and ends with vespers of Easter Sunday.

EVENT, SYMBOL, AND INTERPRETATION

The document interprets the Pasch to mean the passing of the Lord from this world to the Father. There is always some risk involved when an official document adopts one particular interpretation of a polyvalent symbol. The image of passing from this world serves quite well as an interpretation of Christ's death and resurrection and it fitted well, historically, with the catechumenal preparation for baptism, but it would be unfortunate were it to wipe out alternative images that also belong to the history of the triduum and are inherent to at least some parts of the liturgy. One such image presents Christ as the paschal lamb and the pouring out of his blood as the guarantee of redemption from enslavement and the sign of God's covenant. Another celebrates the suffering Christ and his descent into hell as the struggle whereby he gained victory over the powers of darkness and over death itself.

The wording of the document alerts us to the blending of the historical and the symbolic that marks these days. By starting the triduum with the commemoration of the Last Supper and ending it with vespers of Easter Sunday, the celebration moves sequentially through the events being commemorated: the supper with its washing of the feet and the eucharistic command; the betrayal, passion, and death of Friday; the lying in the tomb; the rising from the dead and the Easter appearances. The congregation is keyed into this sequence through the triduum's liturgies and observances. This arrangement is not so much a historicization as it is a necessary memorial of those events in which God's saving action enters human history. By focusing on the particular moments of the passion, people are helped in their devotion to the living Christ as well as in their remembrance of his great love and compassion.

On the other hand, the document observes that it is the mystery and not simply the historical moments being celebrated and that this celebration is done in liturgical signs and sacramentals (no. 38). This statement underscores the symbolic rather than the purely historical nature of all the services, such as the veneration of the cross and the praise of the Easter candle. It is in the nature of a sacramental or symbolic celebration to draw many things into a unity of meaning or to bring the meaning of a sequence of events into particular focus in a single ritual.

Living symbols both gather and scatter meanings. In that sense, the three days offer a congregation a sequence of rites, each of which in its own way draws the congregation to the heart of the redemptive mystery. Thus the washing of the feet as an act of loving service, the veneration of the cross on which Christ triumphed, the watching at the tomb through Saturday's fast, the gathering in the night made bright as day, and the proclamation of the Gospel of the resurrection are each in their own way expressive of the total mystery of the three days. At the moment that each celebration focuses on its key symbolic action, attention is no longer drawn to a sequence of events but to the totality of the mystery as it is celebrated within that symbol.

While the document rightly calls for some suitable catechesis as a means to greater participation (no. 41), it is well to recall that the best catechesis is sensate celebration. The symbolic actions themselves have the power to enlighten and inspire when they succeed in actually drawing people into their celebration by sight, sound, touch, and voice. There is no part of the triduum celebration at which the congregation can be left as spectator or audience. The washing of the feet; the singing of the passion narrative; the veneration of the cross; the praise and procession of the paschal candle; the blessing of the water; the baptismal profession, immersion, and anointing; the welcome of the neophytes into the congregation; and the communion at the eucharistic table—all have the potential to draw the entire congregation into the mystery. Twenty years after Vatican II, it is surely axiomatic to say that the most elaborate explanation draws no participation in faith or hope if it is attached to mean symbols, as it is also true that windy explanations can kill good liturgy on the spot.

A SPACE OF THREE DAYS

It is clear that the Congregation for Divine Worship would like the three days to be a time of Christian reflection and prayer, even of retreat, rather than simply a sequence of harried preparation and breathless rites. It is difficult to realize that goal in today's social circumstances, but the suggestions made in the document may offer at least some possibilities.

The two-day fast is given importance, embracing not only Friday but also Saturday. Psychologically there is nothing like a fast for enforcing the senses and the mind. Instead of linking this fast with the goal of improved health, as so many diets do in a society concentrated on self, the triduum links fasting with meditation on the taking away of the Spouse and the expectation of the resurrection (no. 39). This is a case of retrieving the genuine meaning of the Christian fast as a communion with Christ in his sufferings and thus also as an act of compassion for the world and an expression of eschatological hope. From ancient Christian times, fasting was seen as a preparation for the eucharistic table, as a hunger for the Lord. It was to be broken only in communion, when through the blessed food and drink of Christ's body and blood, one joined fully in the joy and hope of Christ's Pasch. The fast is a primary means to make the entire time of the triduum a participation in the paschal mystery of Christ.

Some other suggestions in the document have to do with times of prayer distinct from the central liturgical actions, by which the three days as a unit of time can become a sacrament of the mystery. The Congregation mentions morning prayer on Good Friday and Saturday, as well as the office of readings, and in so doing it evokes memories (not nostalgic, one hopes) of the office of Tenebrae, with its striking chant and awesome candle ritual. The intention is to offer ways that lead the faithful to meditate on "the passion, death and burial of the Lord while awaiting the announcement of the resurrection" (no. 40).

Obviously these specific suggestions are much more suitable for religious communities and seminaries than they are for the general members of the congregation or for the parish. The desire to provide people with an instrument of meditation, however, should challenge parishes and their pastoral teams. Families might be helped to find ways to spend a few moments together in reading the passion or otherwise meditating on Christ's suffering and compassion. With some volunteer help, other than that of the ministers engaged in the liturgical action, it might be possible to provide a time of collective meditation in the church before the reserved sacrament on Thursday night, a biblical way of the cross on Friday, and short periods of reflection in the parish church in the course of Saturday.

THE QUALITY OF CELEBRATION

Other recommendations in this section of the document have to do with the quality of celebration. Some concern the preparation of the ministers, while others suggest linking smaller congregations in order to provide a more fitting celebration of the services. The proposals that religious communities participate in these services in parish churches and that seminarians (treated here as a breed apart) gather where the bishop is to be found (no. 43) show that we still have to develop approaches to corporate worship that can help undo the division among the baptized, clergy, and religious.

Most of the recommendations about the quality of worship have to do with music and chant (no. 42). Some of the music proposed as desirable belongs to the roles of specific ministers. This is the music for the passion narrative, the Easter proclamation, and the blessings of the water. The congregation's parts that should always be sung are the intercessions and the veneration of the cross on Good Friday. For the congregation at the Vigil, the document mentions the response to the Easter proclamation, the alleluia, the litany of the saints, and the acclamation after the blessing of the water.

The pattern here is one of sung dialogue between minister and people. The sense of chant as a key mode of participation in the central liturgical action is on target, as is the appreciation of the responsorial form. It need only be remarked that we await a development of the sense of other liturgical rites that would see the principle applied more broadly. Thus responsory or acclamation could be built into the blessings of the paschal candle and the baptismal water and even into the chanting of the passion narrative. A model for such dialogue has been supplied in the texts for eucharistic prayers for celebrations with children, but it has still to be followed through in developing all sorts of texts for use with the complete congregation. The triduum would be a great place to start.

Among other chants that deserve attention, processions are given pride of place. Movement and voice go well together in drawing congregations into an action and a mystery. Sometimes a procession originates simply in the need to bring a congregation from one place to another, as after the blessing of the fire and the lighting of the candle at the church entrance during the Vigil or in the brief but significant entrance of the neophytes into the congregation. Sometimes it is set up for its own instrinsic memory or its pilgrimage significance, as with the procession of the palms on Passion Sunday or the procession for venerating the cross on Good Friday. In either case, the accompaniment of movement by participated chant is largely what gives the procession its symbolic power. This fact is better appreciated by people in the traditions of gospel music than by others.

The attention given to two processions on Holy Thursday is curious. The first is the procession with the gifts, highlighted in preference to the washing of feet. The significance attached to this procession has to do with service of the poor (no. 52). If there is one liturgical action that traditionally expresses an attitude of service, and especially service to the poor, it is the Holy Thursday foot washing. In the current ritual, of course, this ceremonial has been turned into a historical reenactment of the washing at the Last Supper, whereas in fact it originated in the monastic and cathedral practice of serving and caring for the poor, especially on this day, in response to the command to do to one another as Christ has done to us.

One of the hardest processions to provide for musically is the one to the place of repose. It is hard to sense the purpose of this reservation and thus of the procession leading to it. If our western heritage were unaccustomed to public sacramental reservation and experienced it only in connection with a eucharist of the presanctified, or if communion from previously consecrated bread were a truly exceptional experience, the situation would be different, and the procession could be compelling. But as it is, the solemnity attached to this act appears to be so much fuss over something not at all unusual; the procession seems to be without a purpose or any intrinsic significance in the sequence of celebrations, and it is hard to make it engaging.

In general, this section of the document draws attention to the organic unity of all the services and to the sacramentality of time itself. Though it appears somewhat narrow in the meaning it attaches to this liturgical sequence, it invites us to reflect on the meaning, taking as our starting point the actual services. It encourages good and careful celebration and an appreciation of the sacramentality of time in asking that the entire space of days be afforded its meaning and be devoted to the memory of the passion and the expectation of the resurrection. It underlines the quality of celebrations in different ways, especially as promoted through careful preparation of the ministers and the use of music. All of this is sage advice that can help congregations focus their efforts at improved celebrations that will be not only performed well, but will be qualitative and spirit-filled.

Eileen Burke-Sullivan

SEVEN

HOLY THURSDAY: NAMING THE ABUSE

Evening . . . bells . . . bread . . . bare feet . . . wine . . . processions . . . glory . . . sorrow . . . *Pangue lingua gloriosi* . . . the poor . . . stillness . . . deepening darkness . . . midnight . . . Holy Thursday begins the sacred triduum with a swirl of images, sounds, moods that form a paradoxical entry into the mystery of our Christian faith. In its "Circular Letter on Preparing and Celebrating the Paschal Feasts" the Congregation for Divine Worship reiterates some important ritual considerations that shape the Holy Thursday liturgy. Since the letter is addressed specifically to the problem of "correcting abuses" in current practice, all of the important ritual considerations are not covered—some are not even mentioned—so someone planning the triduum would find the document helpful only in a context where the fuller treatment of other texts is available.

Some issues of worship continue to trouble parishes, dioceses, or national conferences enough, however, that it is worth considering what the letter addresses as well as what it does not. It is a truism that liturgy shapes, expresses, and catechizes our theology; it is further widely accepted that symbolic language is often more powerful (if somewhat more ambiguous) than verbal language in communicating mystery and faith. It is important, then, that our liturgy, filled as it is with symbolic and verbal language, be done with the utmost care, consideration, and ongoing reflection.

73

On the less positive side, unfortunately, this letter conveys a churlish, hand-slapping tone. The Congregation will receive more cooperation from educated laity and clergy alike when documents are addressed to intelligent adults rather than in a tone of a petulant chiding aimed as if to recalcitrant six-year olds. The tone is unfortunate because it suggests that Roman authority fails to reverence and respect its worldwide community, and because many who might profit by the reminders will most likely ignore the letter as one more impractical and uncaring complaint from people who do nothing real about pastoring in living, vibrant parishes.

Despite its tone the document does offer some valuable reminders, particularly five important issues of concern for preparing and celebrating Holy Thursday. Generally these issues apply to the eucharist in varying degrees of emphasis every time it is celebrated. That makes sense, since celebrating Holy Thursday is about celebrating the eucharistic dimension of the paschal mystery. The five issues are: the pre-eminent role of the community in the celebration; the struggle for the integrity of liturgical signs; the celebration of Christlike service; the relationship of Holy Thursday to the rest of the triduum; and the juxtaposition of solemnity with simplicity and joy with sorrow as they have an impact on worship. And I have to raise one further issue that the document does not address: the size of the worshiping assembly.

Community Pre-eminence

The letter recognizes the importance of the community to the Holy Thursday mystery by reaffirming that the liturgy is to be held at a time in the evening that makes it available to the greatest number of parishioners. Furthermore, an additional celebration is permitted if a sufficiently large number of people want to participate (nos. 46–47). But note that "convenience Masses" for small private groups are not permitted. The document is also clear that priests are not to celebrate the eucharist without a congregation, witnessing to the fact that the eucharist demands the presence of the whole church, not just the clergy (no. 47). The clear message here seems to be that Christ instituted the eucharist for the whole church, and all the baptized believers are commanded to "do this in memory of me."

This ecclesiology is not uniformly upheld in the letter, however, and there is a strong tension with the tradition of celebrating the institution of orders at this Mass as well (nos. 44, 45, 47). For too many centuries the attitude that the eucharist belonged only to the clergy has prevailed, to the terrible detriment of the church, yet the Congregation implies (no. 44) that Christ's "own in the world" are the apostles and their successors in the (ordained) priesthood.

The message that the eucharist is truly given to the whole church could be made clear and uncompromising in the eucharistic celebration by such important symbols as offering communion under the form of wine as well as bread to all communicants and having the foot washing done by the priest and other members of the community for all, or at least for representatives of all in the community. Then the homily might well be given to exploring the mystery of how the baptized must celebrate the eucharist if we are to be true to our vocation as Christians (instead of using this time for explanations, as suggested in no. 45, since that is catechesis, not homiletics.)

The Struggle for Authentic Signs

The struggle for authentic liturgical signs is not unique to the triduum; it should be part of all our work of praising God. But Holy Week deserves special attention because we celebrate so fully that the signs that are most important can be lost because they are most familiar, while our attention is on the galaxy of other, less familiar, symbolic words, gestures, and things.

The Congregation's letter falls into this trap when it is most silent regarding the important fullness of the eucharistic signs. It could have reiterated (but did not) the statement in the General Instruction of the Roman Missal (no. 283) that the "nature of the sign demands that the material for the eucharistic celebration truly have the appearance of food." The bread should look like bread, even though unleavened, in other words. In addition (no. 240 of the General Instruction), "Holy communion has a more complete form when it is received under both kinds . . . Moreover there is a clearer expression of that will by which the new and everlasting covenant is ratified in the blood of the Lord . . . " It would seem to be one of the greatest abuses that even on Holy

Thursday some communities might not have the opportunity of entering fully into the mystery being celebrated because the signs are so weak and inexpressive that the message is lost.

The document does take pains to call for clear and adequate signs surrounding the reservation of the blessed sacrament. The place of reservation is to be simple and dignified, but it should in no way represent a "tomb." The kind of historicity implied in such decorations undermines the whole concept of memorial.

The abuses cited in nos. 49 and 55 indicate further need for education on the difference between active and static manifestations of presence. The triduum models the normative aspects of our worship, so a place of reservation for personal prayer, apart from the place where the asembly gathers to pray communally, should become normative all the time, not just on Holy Thursday. If we grasp the intent of "watching" with the resurrected Christ, we may begin to grasp more fully the Christ in the church who is still suffering.

Another normative practice reaffirmed in this document (no. 48) is that the eucharist given in communion should be consecrated at the Holy Thursday Mass. This certainly challenges our regular practice of providing communion from the tabernacle. The imagery goes back to the passover lamb that had to be completely eaten by the family after it was offered as a sacrifice of praise. Priests know that they must receive communion from the elements consecrated at the present celebration, at least for the sake of legal validity. And for centuries the church has forbidden the practice of regular distribution of preconsecrated elements at the celebration of Mass because it denies the participation of the faithful in this Mass and affirms, once again, that this is the "priest's Mass" alone.

The reaffirmation of the value of the foot washing (no. 51) seems unnecessary except that it appears to reflect a clear intention to correct the "abuse" of anyone except men representing the service of Christian charity at this point. Such petty sexism seems grossly out of place in this letter, and it is a clear slap at the U.S. National Conference of Catholic Bishops, who have requested that the loving service of women be recognized as reflecting the example of Christ. There are two problems with this statement, and the least of them is that the intent seems to be that twelve men recall the historical moment of the foot washing. The problem is that such historicized memorializing is exactly what is forbidden in the strictures against having the place of reservation on this same night resemble a tomb.

The second problem with the limitation of the gesture to "chosen men" is the presumption that this stance, appearing here and in the new Ceremonial of Bishops, reflects a belief that those whose feet are washed can more closely stand in for Jesus and/or the apostles because of their maleness than because of their authentic service. This same line of argument was used in the document on the ordination of women issued some years ago; it is a dangerous argument because it undermines the whole theology of baptism. The command "do this in memory of me," as I mentioned above, was given to the whole church, not only to the ordained successors of the apostles. Church leaders themselves have insisted that all baptized Christians are to "do this"—follow the example of the servant Christ—by serving one another lovingly, carrying for each other's needs and concerns, laying down their own lives for a friend, and taking, eating, and drinking in remembrance. Such commands have not traditionally been applied only to the ordained, but they are constantly taught as the call to holiness for every member of the community of faith (cf. the papal letter *Christifideles Laici*, nos. 14ff).

Celebrating Christlike Service

The focus on service at the Holy Thursday liturgy becomes obvious in the foot washing ceremony, and the letter's affirmation of this ceremony's importance further emphasizes the dimension of service. The letter does not stress the fullness of the ritual sign, unfortunately, for it is important to really do the foot washing, not merely pretend. Washing both feet with real water and drying them is part and parcel of offering service. A symbolic statement loses its power when mere efficiency robs it of its own message.

Service in charity is also emphasized by the collection of money for the poor—preferably the fruit of Lenten fasting—and the sending of the ministers from the assembly to take the eucharist of this celebration to the sick or imprisoned who could not be present (nos. 52, 53). This act unites them to this praying assembly in the body and blood of Christ, but this service is merely a show unless the sick are regularly attended by ministers, and the community understands the importance of bringing the eucharist of this gathering to them.

The loving service of Christ is further exemplified in the Holy Thursday liturgy by those who stay to watch and wait in the presence of the blessed sacrament until midnight. Such watching is a prayer for the faith community and a way of expressing special love to the church by waiting with her and her Lord on this night and in the great night of waiting at the Vigil on Holy Saturday.

Holy Thursday and the Rest of the Triduum

The Holy Thursday liturgy must be seen in its context as the first part of the triduum; the rest of the celebration follows the experience of Holy Thursday, which should set all the "right tones." Such a sense of beginning is created by ringing bells during the singing of the *Gloria* and then stilling them until that hymn is repeated at the Vigil, thus linking these two parts of the whole (no. 50). Furthermore, the instruction limiting the use of instrumental music applies not only to Holy Thursday but also to Good Friday and Holy Saturday, even through the first part of the Vigil.

The omission of the final blessing on Holy Thursday, replacing it by processing with the eucharist to the place of reservation, clearly indicates the "unfinishedness" of the evening liturgy, and bringing communion to the Good Friday liturgy from the Holy Thursday eucharist links the two ceremonies as parts of the same celebration. It is important to note (no. 54) that the transfer of the blessed sacrament is not to occur if the Good Friday liturgy is not being celebrated in the same church on the next day.

Solemnity and Simplicity, Joy and Sorrow

The paradox inherent in every celebration of the eucharist—the sorrow of Jesus' death and the glory of his resurrection—is especially poignant on Holy Thursday. The whole triduum seeks to keep these elements in tension, but Easter moves dramatically to the joy side, and Good Friday into Holy Saturday leans heavily toward the sorrow. Holy Thursday strives to capture both aspects by taking us to the core of the tension created by these conflicting emotions. The joyful ringing of bells as we sing the *Gloria* shortly after a gathering hymn that calls us to glory in the cross of Christ contrasts sharply with the demands of service reflected in more somber music, the scripture readings, and the foot washing ceremony, and it contrasts even more sharply with the sorrow reflected in the somber night of prayer, the simple adornment of the reservation place, and the stripped church. Anyone who truly rides the "spiritual roller coaster" of Holy Thursday indeed knows the hard work that liturgical prayer demands of us.

Megaparish, U.S.A.

The circular letter offers some very helpful reminders about celebrating Holy Thursday, but it does so in response to reported abuses, and that causes the Congregation to emphasize some less important aspects and ignore more important ones. This may leave many people confused about what is really important in the triduum celebration.

As is the case with many documents from Rome, this letter does little or nothing to take into consideration a celebrating community larger than two or three hundred people. In the community I serve we regularly gather between five and six thousand people each Sunday, and nearly ten thousand of us gather for Easter, with only two resident priests. These facts have a definite impact on the way we prepare and celebrate the paschal feasts.

The "megaparish" is relatively new, but it will not be long in spreading to more and more dioceses. Yet little or nothing is being written about ways to adapt the ritual that must necessarily take place in such large congregations. As liturgist in our ever-growing parish (we presently have over 150 inquirers, candidates, and catechumens in the RCIA process), I am convinced that intensive study of the rites and the theology behind them is urgent if we are to make adaptations that give life to our celebrations. Clarifications from the Congregation for Divine Worship are needed and welcome as part of that process, and the correction of genuine abuses will help the universal church retain her unity of worship. One would hope that the authors of such documents take the time to participate in the celebrations they are seeking to correct, so that they truly understand the nature of the faith community they are attempting to serve.

Tim Schoenbachler

EIGHT

GOOD FRIDAY: SOME ALTERNATE SUGGESTIONS

You might call the Congregation of Divine Worship's ritual directives for Good Friday "Getting Back to Basics." While there is very little added to the present order as found in the sacramentary, there is a notable re-emphasis of particular elements that have been in place since the 1955 revision of Holy Week—important gestures and symbols, rich in their beauty and grace, which are significant to the Good Friday celebration's power to communicate and express our faith and feelings about the paschal event. What one senses in these directives, then, is a concern for present practice.

The most notable points of re-emphasis are the initial prostration of the ministers (no. 65), the concern that the homily "should be" given (no. 66)—as opposed to "may be" in the sacramentary; the reassertion of the full list of intercessions (no. 67; evidently some are being excised, altered, or added to by local churches); and the personal adoration of *one* cross (nos. 68–69—note, not a crucifix), as opposed to the present option of using additional crosses if the number of those venerating is large.

FAMILIARITY vs. CREATIVITY

The emphasis placed on these "ancient traditions," as the Congregation calls them, reminds us of an important truth about

81

ritual. Good ritual often relies on familiarity with the gestures, words, and symbols, as well as the ways they are opened up to our senses and experience.

We may wish, therefore, to give some thought to what "creativity" means as we approach our preparation for the assembly's ritual. Creativity does not necessarily mean "reinventing the wheel" each year. By its nature the Good Friday liturgy is unique, and though it is celebrated only once a year, people remember its particular actions and gestures. They are simple and powerful, especially when done well. The elements presented to us for this liturgy provide a fitting way to celebrate our Savior's death and resurrection. Yet the Congregation's letter implies that people are writing their own ritual, and in doing so are opting to delete or downplay elements that are traditionally important to the nature of the celebration.

After a few years of planning Good Friday at my last parish, we arrived at a way of celebrating the established elements that touched the heart of the paschal mystery. More importantly, the liturgy touched people—and they told us so. It was good. That liturgy is now a parish tradition, and every year the community looks forward to that ritual moment because they remember it. The people can enter into the liturgy, and their familiarity with its structure frees them to celebrate with mind and heart and spirit. They do not have to be concerned with what's next or what we're going to do now, which can so often be the undoing of celebration.

The wrong attitude to creativity is personified in a presider who is compelled to begin each part of the service with this statement: "Now we are going to (ritual element named), by which we (ritual element explained); so let us (choreographic direction.)" One can imagine what such commentary does to prayer. A worship aid that does the same thing in print is not much better, because it keeps the faithful glued to the "aid"—a misnomer in this case. Such printed commentaries are not a help but an apology for leading people through the unfamiliar waters of a "new and improved" liturgy. Good liturgy speaks for itself; traditions take root. Familiarity can free people to pray and to experience the mystery.

LIFT HIGH THE CROSS

When one thinks of the Good Friday liturgy, the veneration of the cross rightly comes to mind as the most memorable element. It is the most dramatic part of the ritual, as personal as it is communal. As we ponder and celebrate the mystery of the cross, that powerful symbol not only moves us to triumphant joy at our Savior's victory, it also becomes a catharsis for our own suffering and death as Christ's mystery penetrates our lives and illuminates our human experience.

The document speaks of using a single cross of "appropriate size and beauty" (no. 68). "Size" and "beauty" are relative terms. Scale relates to the entire worship space, the distance from the symbol to the assembly and the relationship to the human scale. "Beauty" does not relate to the materials of which the cross is made; the "old, rugged cross" can certainly be beautiful. The truly "beautiful" evokes a response, either positive or negative, and leads the beholder to penetrate on a deeper level that which is actually seen.

The sacramentary states: "In the United States, more crosses may be used, if the number venerating is large." I have found this compromise disappointing (and it seems that the Congregation agrees); it undermines the power of the symbol and the action of the entire assembly approaching one cross, especially as the additional ones are usually smaller and visually less attractive.

The Congregation's letter asks us to ponder the choice between experience and expedience. This is where true creativity is called for. How can a large number of people venerate a single cross and do so for a duration that does not become burdensome or cause the liturgy to bog down? I offer this possibility for your consideration. What if the cross were so made that it could be easily taken apart in two or three pieces, so that all could venerate it during the service? For people who want to spend more time meditating privately on the mystery of the cross, the document offers some suggestions for private veneration of the cross after the Good Friday service, continuing even through the day on Saturday (nos. 71, 74, 76).

The Congregation refers to the communion rite on Good Friday as *an* "ancient tradition," and so it is, but it is not the *most* ancient tradition. Some of the suggestions made about the communion rite can actually continue the dramatic nature of the service of veneration. It is recommended, for instance, that the Lord's Prayer be sung (a familiar melody, please). If the parish does not normally make some gesture during this prayer—holding hands or raising hands together—this might be a good day to encourage such action, since the people gathered for the Holy Week services are usually there because they want to be and are therefore a bit more homogeneous and involved in the service. Is not vocal participation much better generally on these days? It is interesting that Adrian Nocent points out in *The Liturgical Year* (2:72) a connection between the veneration of the cross and the communion rite. "According to the old Ordo 31," he writes, "the faithful kissed the cross immediately before receiving communion. The adoration of the cross and the reception of communion were thus brought into close proximity and became, in effect, a single action."

Communion on Good Friday normally consists of sharing the bread consecrated on Holy Thursday. Nowhere have I experienced the wine being reserved and shared on Friday, but this is certainly a possibility: wine can easily be stored overnight. The shedding of Christ's blood is a central image of the day, and there could be great benefit in the symbol of the shared cup as we celebrate the "blood of the lamb" poured out.

The document's language certainly suggests a triumphant celebration of the cross, "carried out with the splendor of the mystery of our salvation" (no. 68). This seems contrary to the usual approach to Good Friday as "the day Christ died." Indeed we do remember and celebrate Christ's death, yet we are ever aware as a post-resurrection people that this event was neither defeat nor destruction, but our salvation and glory. When we celebrate the Christ mystery we do not so much remember the historical events as to look to their deeper significance and meaning. This is our reason for joy and celebration. The texts to be sung during the veneration of the cross, even the "reproaches," speak to this triumphant mood.

Friday is a day of great and mixed emotions, so there may be some confusion about what we should be feeling. The Congregation's letter seems to handle the confusion by separating the emphasis—triumph on Friday, with Saturday picking up the underlying sorrowful tone of the preceding day. Yet the rite as we now have it, and even the Congregation's description, "flip-flops" between sadness and joy. This indecision attests to the reality that these emotions cannot be easily separated or even manipulated to apply to precise moments. Sorrow and joy, after all, are frequently one reality in lived experience, and the cross itself embodies the breadth of these emotions. Such mixed emotions, then, are not some kind of liturgical schizophrenia in need of correction, but life—our life and Jesus' life—as we experience it in its fullness.

If we do arrange our services to move from triumph on Friday to sorrow on Saturday, from veneration of the exalted cross to a stripped church building in which we watch "as it were at the Lord's tomb" (no. 73), we may find the order of emotions unlikely, but do we not repeat this order every time we celebrate a funeral liturgy? Family and church gather in the midst of their grief to celebrate the triumph of resurrection, but people surely leave the funeral Mass with mixed emotions, and they finally end the rite at a very potent and emotional station: the grave.

Hope and joy do not diminish our grief and sense of loss or tragedy. We would never deny these feelings to the grieving family, nor does the church's ritual deny them to us, Christ's "spouse" (no. 58). Indeed, any good ritual does not seek to define or limit the range of our human response. It provides a framework by which we are enabled to enter into the mystery with our hearts, minds, spirit, and faith; it allows us to express and experience the full breadth of our faith and feelings.

On the face of it, Good Friday appears to be a day marked by a simplicity of symbol and action, yet it is quite complex in meaning and emotion. The day itself symbolizes the irony of life's opposites. The Congregation for Divine Worship, in re-emphasizing the care to be taken with the prescribed symbols, actions, and gestures, reminds us of the potency in good ritual brought to life by the assembly and its ministers.

Ronald E. Brassard

NINE

EASTER VIGIL: "PERFORMED IN ALL THEIR FULLNESS AND NOBILITY . . . "

Whenever I hear that there is a new document from Rome, I shudder. In this time when a new rubricism seems to be creeping up everywhere, it is easy to suspect that another Roman document will mean nothing more than repressive directives that take two steps backward for every step forward. I am happy that this is not the case with the circular letter on "Preparing and Celebrating the Paschal Feasts." And nowhere is that happy truth more evident than in the section dealing with Holy Saturday and the celebration of the Easter Vigil. My task is to explore what that section of the document is about and to flesh out some of its very worthwhile suggestions.

The person who reads this letter quickly, without a great deal of reflection, might be struck by the negative language in this section. But do not be fooled; there is good reasoning behind the carefully chosen phrases. Many abuses of this most sacred of vigils have occurred over the past years. I remember giving a workshop at a parish in the midwest where the Vigil was celebrated at 5:00 P.M. on Holy Saturday night, long before the sun had set. When I discussed this practice with the parish staff, their attitude betrayed the American malaise of efficiency and lack of appreciation for the symbolic power of this, or perhaps any, celebration. While the example is extreme, it suggests the wider lack of respect for symbol and ritual prevalent in far too many parishes.

87

This section of the document tries to combat these abuses by stressing smooth, full, and noble celebrations of the rites as the best way to communicate their meaning (no. 82). The instructions point out the need to recover carefully the celebration's meaning as a time of waiting and preparation for the Lord's resurrection and as a time to celebrate the sacraments of Christian initiation (no. 77). After pointing out the noble character of this Vigil and issuing careful instructions that under no circumstances should it begin before the setting of the sun (no. 78), the letter offers a careful analysis of the celebration's four sections.

A Noble Beginning

The words describing the first part of the ritual are so beautiful they are worth repeating: "The first part consists of symbolic acts and gestures which require that they be performed in all their fullness and nobility so that their meaning, as explained by the opening words of the celebrant and the liturgical prayers, may be truly understood by the faithful" (no. 82). These words, combined with the next three paragraphs, give pastors, liturgists, and musicians a great deal to chew on.

The fire first. Ideally, it should be located outside the church and be large enough that it truly "dispels the darkness." It is time to stop lighting small hibachis at the head of the main aisle in a semidarkened church. Let the rich burning of the fire break into the night; let the fire be lit so that as people approach the church they can see it proclaiming the beginning of our freedom celebration. One prominent liturgical designer has suggested that a special place—a rather large stone bowl—be set up permanently with a plaque on it that describes this as the place where the Easter fire is lit.

Presiders need to take great care to proclaim the rich and powerful words that accompany this opening ritual in a manner befitting the text. Their enthusiasm must surely be stronger than that of the announcer who tells us that "Flight No. 707 is now ready for boarding." The rich language of the Vigil demands an energy worthy of proclaiming that the feast of liberation is at hand.

The document only hints at the quality of the Easter candle, but here is an opportunity for real artistry and craft. There is no need to purchase the "$29.95-off-the-rack model" when people in the parish might make a candle that would be much worthier of the celebration and more reflective of the character of the people who gather.

Musicians need to fine-tune their craft for the procession, its attending chants, and the singing of the Easter proclamation. Here the document shines. It speaks of extending acclamations and of looking for more ways to involve the assembly in the Easter proclamation. A rich collection of compositions already tries to do this. Musicians need to explore setting of the procession and the Easter proclamation by Everet Freese, Marty Haugen, and Tom Conry (to name but a few). Of particular interest is Tom Conry's introduction to his setting of the Easter Proclamation (Oregon Catholic Press): it is quite effective when chanted as the procession of ministers approaches the new fire.

Liturgists have ample room to explore ways to involve the assembly more intimately in the procession of light. One example: those who gather might prepare their own candles to be lit at this time and again for the renewal of baptismal promises.

Ancient Recollections, Present Proclamation

The opening ritual begs for the fullness of symbolic gesture, but it is really a preliminary act leading to the second part of the Vigil, the celebration of the word of God. This is when we tell our story from ancient recollection to resurrection proclamation. The restored order gives ample opportunity for pastoral planning according to the needs and situations of the individual communities gathered for celebration.

Strong emphasis is placed on the musical nature of the responses and the need for contemporary composers to bring their best efforts to bear on these texts. The goal is not simply singing for the sake of singing, of course—getting through the texts by using a melody based on psalm tone 8G to do the job. Rather, musicians must search out the very best compositions for these psalms, settings that not only serve their liturgical function well but also highlight the integrity of the musical craft.

The document suggests ringing bells at the Glory to God. Once again, parishes can explore a fuller, richer use of that symbolism. Instead of limiting the ringing to the efforts of two altar servers, why not ring many bells located throughout the church? Better yet, why not do as some parishes do, and invite the entire assembly to bring bells from home to add to the festivity?

When it describes intoning the Easter Alleluia, the letter suggests that the presider do this in the traditional way. It is quick to point out, however, that this function can also be done by the cantor. At such a dramatic moment, let the person with the better gift of song be entrusted with this important service to the worshiping assembly.

Cascading Waters

Following the homily (and there should be one, even if it is brief—no. 87), we begin the third part of the celebration, the baptismal liturgy. As always in preparation for this night, careful planning is in order here. The crucial matter is that the rites demand a rich use of water: be lavish in using this central symbol of the resurrection and of this vigil celebration. A simple but effective method of highlighting the water while the presider prays its blessing is to have a deacon or an assisting minister lift the water in their hands and let it fall back again and again like a cascading waterfall.

The renewal of baptismal promises and the attendant sprinkling of the congregation must be done with care. Ministers must walk to everyone and sprinkle everyone. Let the renewal of baptismal promises really become the crowning moment of all the preparations in the Lenten season.

Not in Haste

The treatment of the final section of the celebration—the eucharist—begins at no. 90. The letter highlights the fact that this part above all must not be "celebrated in haste" (no. 91), for despite all that has gone before, this is the "high point" of the Vigil, the "Easter sacrament" par excellence (no. 90). The temptation to be most efficient runs strong here, but when efficiency takes over, it is clear that planning has been poor. A decision to use Eucharistic Prayer II and dash through the remainder of the liturgy indicates that the planners have not looked at celebrating the whole Vigil. If the whole is ever greater than the sum of its parts, that is the case here, and the whole must be considered during the planning process.

In accord with its command not to celebrate in haste, the document suggests singing the eucharistic prayer. Thankfully, composers are doing some serious work in this area. In a similar vein, this section of the letter is very clear and strong about the appropriateness of communion under both species.

Weaknesses and Strengths

If there is a weakness in the document's section on the Easter Vigil, it is in the area of commentaries and explanations. Several things need to be kept in mind about spoken or printed commentaries. The first is that nothing teaches as well as good ritual done with care and filled with conviction. The second is that explanations of the entire paschal celebration can be presented well in advance of ceremonies through good use of the parish bulletin. And the third point is that any comments made during the celebration should be governed by the great and important rule, "Less is more."

The strength of this letter lies in three areas. First, it gives strong backing to maintaining the integrity of the Vigil celebration. Second, it strongly supports the use of good music and creativity in music. Third, it puts the Easter Vigil in perspective. I think that one of the problems we are beginning to encounter is an overtaking of the full celebration of Easter by the celebration of the Vigil. The Vigil is the central celebration of the resurrection, of course, but it should not subsume the full celebration of Easter Sunday as the day of victory or the "Great Sunday" of the fifty days of the Easter Season. What we do in the nightwatch on Holy Saturday is the completion of the Lenten journey and the high point of the triduum, but it is also the great gateway to the rest of Easter Sunday and the Easter season.

TEN

EASTER DAY & EASTER TIME: BEGINNING TO MAKE THE FIFTY DAYS COME ALIVE

Great credit and thanks should be given to those who have participated in restoring the true meaning of Lent and the triduum. Much the same now needs to be done with the fifty days of Easter, and this letter is a modest contribution to that process. We are substantially better at anticipating something than celebrating the ongoingness of the event. This truth is manifested throughout western cultures where the bride and groom often leave halfway through the reception, to the American Christmas, which begins before Thanksgiving and ends promptly on December 25th.

So we have maintained a great and substantial theoretical understanding of the importance of the Easter season, but in practice we do not have an ongoing religious celebration of Easter. One possible reason for this up to the present, in addition to our cultural practices, has been the absence of neophytes, whose presence would make the traditions we have inherited make sense. Easter is the postbaptismal season, but for centuries we have tried to live Easter without baptism.

The circular letter from the Congregation for Divine Worship does a fine job of commenting on what takes place up to and including the celebration of the Easter Vigil, but it is much sketchier in discussing the Easter season, and it raises many more questions than it answers. Approaching the season this way is honest, and the Congregation is to be commended, for it cannot comment well on a subject so underdeveloped and ripe for exploration. What it does say gives the needed exploration both the impetus and direction we should expect from this Congregation.

Easter Comes Despite Exhaustion

Three paragraphs of the letter (nos. 97–99) deal with Easter Sunday itself. They comment on the importance of the day continuing the celebration of the night before and emphasize, as the letter also does in no. 82, the significant position in which the paschal candle is to be placed.

What these paragraphs cannot comment upon is the reality of exhausted ministers, tired from days of planning and celebration, who must draw on deeply held resources to be "up" for Easter Sunday celebrations that are almost anticlimactic for them. Yet these services are Easter for vast numbers of people, for merged with the faithful are those who come to church on this day, but on few others. All too often what these people experience is a Mass with missing ministers, tired homilists, and used music. Or everything is done so well that it is clear that in this parish the Easter Vigil was not treated as the focus of the Easter celebration, but only a regular Saturday night Mass.

Parishes must devote great time and attention to Easter Sunday with the honest realization that the community gathered for these celebrations is not the same community that has celebrated the Easter Vigil. Those places that have created a special core of people who treat Easter Sunday morning as a unique opportunity for evangelizing, hospitality, care, and concern have done well in bringing a new meaning to the renewal of baptismal promises on that day.

As we continue working to bring the beautiful and powerful Easter Vigil to full prominence, we cannot allow Easter Sunday to fall into decline. The fact is, however, that with rare exceptions the same people who lead the triduum will not have the strength to minister well on Easter Sunday

Business as Usual

The letter places a mild stress on the importance of the Sundays of Easter (nos. 100–101), but with one exception there is barely a mention of the Easter octave. These facts reflect the sad reality that there are few places that do more after Easter Sunday than revert back to the regular weekday schedules existing before Ash Wednesday. We can change that reality, but to do so requires us to look very differently at what the Easter weekday celebrations should be and should include—certainly during the week between Easter and "Low" Sunday (the Second Sunday of Easter). At the very least, one way to begin making the octave of Easter different than other weeks is to celebrate the liturgy of the hours.

The letter's comments on the Easter Sundays include this statement: "Celebrations in honor of the Blessed Virgin Mary or the saints which fall during the week may not be transfered to one of these Sundays" (no. 101). While the Congregation is most likely pinpointing groups that have May traditions honoring Mary, the statement applies to other traditions as well, such as the way we celebrate Mother's Day in the United States. On the one hand, Mother's Day does not appear as a feast in the liturgical calendar, so it should not interfere with the Sunday celebration. On the other hand, it is probably an event being celebrated or commemorated in one way or another by all the people attending Mass that day, so there is pressure to include this theme in the liturgy. There is no easy answer to the problem; these secular feasts and their liturgical impact need much more study.

Mystagogia, the Missing Feast, and Other Practices

The materials about the neophytes and the importance of mystagogia are not long enough or strong enough (nos. 102–103). They do not even make the obvious and important connection between the assigned lectionary readings for the season and the ongoing postbaptismal instruction that must be directed not only to the newly baptized but to all the faithful who form the postbaptismal community.

As a parish priest for many years, I firmly believe that the homilies of the Easter season must be—and can be—among the best given throughout the year. I do not want to suggest that preachers should ever skimp on preparation, but the realities contained in the Easter season readings are so vibrant and contemporary that they call out, challenging homilists to excellence. Just as we are rediscovering that Lent is a season that comes to life because of the rituals and process of adult initiation, so we are beginning to rediscover that the fifty days of Easter unfold their deepest treasures when seen through the eyes of those who are newly baptized.

The last sentence of no. 103 and all of no. 104 deal with communion in the Easter season. The celebration of first communion in its present form can be done well on a Sunday in this season, but it must be a celebration that harks back to the intrinsic connection among the services of the triduum and expresses well the total reality that is the eucharist. Most of no. 104 deals with the "Easter duty" of receiving communion once during the season— not so much of a problem in these days of frequent communion and a restored sense of the place of communion in the eucharist as it once was. The only mention of the Easter octave appears in this paragraph: a suggestion that communion be brought to the sick during this special week. There is also some good advice here about home visitation and private devotions (nos. 105–106).

An astonishing omission appears at this point in the letter. There is no mention of the feast of the Lord's Ascension. Such absence of any reference to this feast must be a mistake, but all too often such an omission appears as well in parish liturgical planning. The Ascension is a powerful feast that lends itself to good celebration. In a certain way it is what an old priest once called a "doctrinal feast," one that celebrates Christian belief rather than a specific historical event, and so it can be linked with the post-Pentecostal "doctrinal feasts" of Trinity Sunday and the Solemnity of Christ's Body and Blood.

The paragraph on Pentecost (no. 107) is again too brief to be of much aid, except for its interesting emphasis on the Pentecost Vigil rather than liturgy on the day itself. The letter calls for a "prolonged celebration of the Mass in the form of a vigil whose character is not baptismal . . . but is one of urgent prayer . . . " "Urgent prayer" could be an excellent description of how Christians can and should pray for our concerns and the world around us, but I must admit that I do not know how the character of urgent prayer differs from other prayer, despite the suggestions made in the footnote. Are we being invited to experiment with an all-night prayer, or forms of dance, or new modes of adoration, or what?

The RCIA calls for the close of postbaptismal catechesis "at the end of the Easter season near Pentecost Sunday" with "some sort of celebration" (RCIA no. 249). The rite leaves lots of room for creativity, suggesting only that "festivities in keeping with local custom may accompany the occasion." The circular letter paraphrases that statement (no. 103). It adds no further suggestions, but the paraphrase causes a problem, for it contains the phrase "on or about Pentecost Sunday." The RCIA is fairly clear that whatever celebrations take place, they should not necessarily fall on Pentecost itself.

The letter concludes with two quotations that offer further possibilities for pastoral reflection and development, but they also reflect the problems this letter poses. The first is a quotation from St. Leo the Great reminding us that the "whole church rejoices at the forgiveness of sins" (no. 108). Leo says that this festival celebration of forgiveness applies to the newly baptized and also to "those who have long been numbered among the adopted children," but the letter gives no indication how this theme should be integrated or expressed in the Easter season.

And repeating the themes that have run through this whole letter, its authors adapt some phrases from the opening prayer for Saturday of Easter's seventh week to say: "By means of a more intensive pastoral care and a deeper spiritual effort, all who celebrate the Easter feasts will by the Lord's grace experience their effects in their daily lives." That intensified pastoral care and deeper spiritual effort could have used some more practical advice than what is offered here. In the end this is a good letter, a good beginning—but only a beginning—in the necessary renewal of the Easter season.

THE MUSIC

David Hollier

ELEVEN

CHOOSING MUSIC FOR THE RITES

Recently I participated in a workshop on "Music and the RCIA" offered to musicians in a Pennsylvania diocese. The turnout was a little disappointing for those who planned the day, but I explained that part of the problem is that musicians are not concerned with the RCIA. They do not experience it as a liturgical rite, but as something that the DRE or the catechist does. Musicians do not yet see how important their role is in the development of this ritual process for their particular parish community. It is essential that musicians read and study the ritual's text and introductory material. J. Michael McMahon's *Liturgical Commentary on the RCIA* is an excellent help in understanding the rite.[1] In this article I am going to explore the various roles played by musicians and music at three points in the RCIA: the rite of acceptance into the order of catechumens, the rite of election, and the scrutinies.

Rite of Acceptance into the Order of Catechumens

The earliest record of this rite appears in the *Apostolic Tradition* of Hippolytus (Rome, third century C.E.). Inquirers were brought before the assembled people to state their intentions; sponsors also testified on their behalf. The RCIA echoes this history:

Assemblying publicly for the first time, the candidates who have completed the period of the precatechumenate declare their intention to the Church and the Church in turn, carrying out its apostolic mission, accepts them as persons who intend to become its members. God showers his grace on the candidates, since the celebration manifests their desire publicly and marks their reception and first consecration by the Church.[2]

One of the first things to note is that this rite of acceptance calls specifically for a number of acclamations that involve the whole community in the prayer after the candidate's first acceptance of the Gospel and in the gestures of signing with the cross and entry into the assembly for the liturgy of the word (nos. 53, 55–56, 60). While there are a fair number of acclamations already in a pastoral musician's repertoire that may set the given texts, acclamations that fit into and express the ritual moments of this rite are hard to find.

Even more difficult to locate are acclamations that are not absolutely required, but which are almost necessary as a way to involve the congregation supportively in the candidate's very first public affirmation of the search for faith, in response to the questions "What do you ask of God's Church?" and "What does faith offer you?"[3] This is a time for the congregation to speak to the inquirer-to-be-catechumen (soon to be called a "candidate") about the community's support, affirmation, and acceptance. The acclamations must be simple, powerful, easily remembered, and easily taught to the assembly.

Another time when singing is not specified in the rite but is certainly useful is in response to the presider's question to the sponsor and the assembly about their readiness "to help these candidates find and follow Christ" (no. 53). The same acclamation could be used instead of a simple "We are." Such sensitivity to the moments in the rite puts flesh on the bare bones of the ritual. Certain moments, in other words, call for musical involvement by the assembly.

The ritual signing of the senses is a moment that can combine song and gesture in a way that makes the whole assembly part of what is going on, not merely silent (or even singing!) spectators. As the various parts of the body are named by the presider, the candidates are signed with the cross of Christ by their sponsors. The rite suggests that all gather outside the church for the first part of the rite, but some places adapt the rite so that the questions and affirmations by the sponsors and assembly are done outside the worship space, with the signing of the senses reserved until after the homily, inside the building. Some parishes use the aisles as well as the sanctuary for this signing, so that it happens throughout the worship space. This is especially effective if there are a number of candidates. It is very important that the touch be effective in the signing of the senses; sponsors should use their whole hand and not limit the touch to the thumb, as the rite says. (Jim Dunning speaks of the "Catholic" thumb.)

David Haas has provided a simple and powerful acclamation for this ritual moment, to be repeated for each signing: "Christ will be your strength! Learn to know and follow him."[4] Another suitable alternative to the text provided would be one of the memorial acclamations used in the parish, such as a setting of "Lord, by your cross and resurrection, you have set us free. You are the savior of the world!" Whatever acclamation is chosen, it must reflect the ritual action and be short enough for the ritual to keep flowing. If the refrain is too long, it simply gets in the way of the action. The purpose is to allow the assembly to respond and be a part of the ritual action, for the assembly's response and involvement are essential to the nature of the catechumenate, which always takes place "within the community of the faithful" (RCIA no. 4).

One other comment about this rite of acceptance is in order: the rite can be repeated several times each year. I recently read an article suggesting that this rite be celebrated annually on the First Sunday of Advent. That needs to be reconsidered, because initiation is a journey in which some rites, at least, cannot be tied to a particular Sunday, even the first Sunday of the liturgical year. The rite of acceptance can—and probably should—be celebrated several times a year, depending on the life journey of each inquirer. Some inquirers may indeed be ready to enter the catechumenate at the beginning of Advent, but others may not be ready until January or even Lent. The whole thrust of the RCIA is that the process of coming to faith "varies according to the many forms of God's grace, the free cooperation of individuals, the action of the Church, and the circumstances of time and place" (RCIA no. 5).[5]

Election

Unlike the rite of acceptance into the catechumenate, the rite of election normally happens on a particular day, the First Sunday of Lent:

> Thus the Church makes its "election," that is, the choice and admission of those catechumens who have the dispositions that make them fit to take part, at the next major celebration, in the sacraments of initiation.

> This step is called election because acceptance made by the Church is founded on the election by God in whose name the Church acts.[6]

Musically, wonderful things can happen in this rite. The rite must be studied carefully, so that a community can choose among the various options and the possibilities offered in the combined rites (Appendix I). The comments here presume the "normal" situation in which the rite of election is celebrated at the cathedral, with the bishop presiding. Since this rite "is the focal point of the Church's concern for the catechumens . . . [a]dmission to election therefore belongs to the bishop . . . " (RCIA no. 121).

What a marvelous and glorious time to celebrate liturgy! People gather from all over the diocese, coming from different ethnic and creedal backgrounds, meeting each other after journeying as catechumens for a period of time. There are various excellent options for gathering songs ("Jesus, Remember Me" from Taizé or the hymn "How Firm a Foundation"), the responsorial psalm after the first reading (Marty Haugen's setting of Psalm 91, "Be with Me, Lord," or one of the numerous settings of Psalm 51 (e.g., Proulx, Kreutz, Roff). Tom Conry's "Hold Us in Your Mercy" is also a very fine piece for this rite.[7]

A very important ritual moment on this occasion is the signing of the book of the elect. There are a number of fine acclamations that can be used at this time. In dioceses where the rite of election is a multicultural occasion, the music reflects this fact. Afro-American, Vietnamese, and Spanish selections are standard parts of the fabric of the rite of election in many dioceses around the country. Here music does not create a "smorgasbord" liturgy; rather, music becomes the mirror reflecting the people gathered. With that image in mind, many of the polylingual songs from Taizé would fit well into such a liturgy.

Scrutinies

The scrutinies, celebrated on the Third, Fourth, and Fifth Sundays of Lent, are extremely powerful rites in their simplicity. They should be, for they have a weighty purpose:

> The scrutinies are meant to uncover, then heal all that is weak, defective, or sinful in the hearts of the elect; to bring out, then strengthen all that is upright, strong, and good. For the scrutinies are celebrated in order to deliver the elect from the power of sin and Satan, to protect them against temptation, and to give them strength in Christ, who is the way, the truth, and the life.[8]

And Robert Duggan puts these ceremonies in context with this description of the Lenten retreat:

> Lent is a special, sacred time in which there is a heightened sense of expectation and openness to the spiritual realities involved in the great drama of redemption. The lenten retreat which is punctuated on three successive Sundays by these powerful prayers for deliverance and healing provides the supportive framework and focus for understanding the meaning of the scrutinies. As the elect approach . . . full initiation, the church pours out her most powerful prayer for God's grace.[9]

The simple but strong structure of the scrutinies demands music that is powerful, assertive, bold, but not elaborate. The environment must be stark, and the music must help create this mood. The lighting might be dim; the use of incense would be appropriate. A number of hymns and psalms can help to create the appropriate context for the scrutinies. One good selection is the hymn "Come, My Way, My Truth, My Life" (Herbert/Williams). Other possibilities include "Amazing Grace," "The Living God My Shepherd Is," "What Wondrous Love Is This," "Be with Me, Lord" (Haugen), and "Parce, Domine."

The prayer for the elect is very important; it is a litany and should be done with great intensity and drive. A very short refrain, such as one of the Taizé "Kyrie eleison" responses, would allow the assembly to participate. But most important, the litany should reflect the struggles of the elect. Musicians and liturgists should spend some time with the elect and their catechist(s) before the scrutinies begin, so they can understand the struggles and the evils from which the elect are praying for deliverance.

That way the intercessions and their musical presentation can be crafted "to fit the various circumstances" (RCIA no. 153).

Now that we have the official text of the RCIA, we can continue and even intensify the search for music that is appropriate for the rites. Musicians need to try some things and evaluate them afterwards, talk things over with the parish catechumenate director and the homilist for the various events. These people will be able to share important insights with a musician or liturgists who is unsure of the appropriateness of certain music selections to reflect and express the rites.

Notes

1. Washington, D.C.: Federation of Diocesan Liturgical Commissions.
2. Rite of Christian Initiation of Adults (RCIA) no. 41.
3. David Haas has produced a very helpful and well-written collection of psalms and acclamations for the RCIA. In *Who Calls You by Name—Music for Christian Initiation* (GIA) is an acclamation to support candidates after they respond to the two questions: "We stand with you, we pray for you, O holy child of God." Michael Joncas' refrain, "I have loved you with an everlasting love, I have called you and you are mine" (*Glory and Praise*, NALR; *Gather*, GIA) is also a good choice for this acclamation.
4. This acclamation is offered as "another suitable acclamation" instead of the one mentioned in the text: "Glory and praise to you, Lord Jesus Christ" (no. 55). The text by Haas is drawn from the interim translation of the rite and echoes the presider's comment: "It is Christ himself who now strengthens you with this sign of his love. Learn to know him and follow him." Haas has also provided an instrumental fragment to be played while the presider announces the next signation. This helps with the continuity and musical flow of the ritual action.
5. See also no. 18 and National Statute 6 (RCIA Appendix III).
6. RCIA no. 119.
7. On these and other suggestions, see the next chapter, by David Haas, in this volume.
8. RCIA no. 141. The penitential rite (scrutiny) on the Second Sunday of Lent for the baptized but uncatechized adults should have the same stark strength; see the RCIA, Part II, Chapter 4D.
9. Robert J. Duggan, *Catechumenate* (July 1988).

David Haas

TWELVE

LITURGICAL GLUE

The Rite of Christian Initiation of Adults is about prophecy and conversion, not only for catechumens and candidates, but for the whole church. The RCIA, and the journey of faith that it heralds, is a reflecting centerpiece for the church's necessary inventory regarding its gospel mission to be light and life for the world. This prophetic stance is intrinsic to the liturgical rites of the catechumenate, and the nature of these rites calls pastoral musicians to rediscover and commit themselves to the formative role of music in worship.

Practically speaking, if the RCIA is going to fulfill its potential to evangelize and renew the body of Christ, then the liturgy must be given priority and sensitivity in its preparation and execution. It follows that the minister of music must become well informed in the rite, understand the various stages of this journey and the rites that are at the center of these stages, and develop the necessary musical skills and knowledge of resources to help ensure that these celebrations not become private ceremonies for a few, but gatherings of prayer and praise for the entire people of God. Above all other things, the RCIA is primarily a *rite*, and music needs to be taken seriously as a force that can help embody the power of these celebrations and service as a vehicle of formation for those embarking on the journey of the Christian life.

While the principle is important for all sacramental celebrations, the liturgies of the catechumenate help us to see more intensely the difference between singing *at* the liturgy and *singing the liturgy*. We musicians lift high the belief that, when something is sung, it holds a greater power and meaning than when it is merely recited. We recognize the *affective* power of music. In a worship experience too often void of this aspect of our faith, the rites of the RCIA are doomed to fail in their call and purpose. Music must more and more become the genre in which these liturgical texts are presented; we need to disclose the truth that liturgy in its very essence is *sung* prayer.

The issues, I believe, are twofold. The first is that we pastoral musicians must function more as the ministers of "liturgical glue." Music must serve as the expression of communal worship, rather than providing musical intermissions between the liturgical actions. Liturgical music must be seen and used as an agent of communication, pacing, and presentation of liturgical prayer.

Practically speaking, improvisational skills are needed where music helps to "connect" by providing transitions and a context in which the rituals and symbols take place. These skills include everything from the ability to play and improvise quietly under the presider's spoken text to helping build and pace the occurence of acclamations and litanies, providing a flow that gives the rite coherence and clarity. The skills involved are musical and liturgical; that is to say, musical improvisational gifts are welcome and necessary elements, but they must be joined to a good knowledge of the rites, a knowledge of how and when music is to be used to help stage and underscore the high and low energy points in the rite.

In the rites of the RCIA, as in all the sacramental rites, these skills are just as important as the ability to play a hymn, if not more so. There are many ritual actions: declaration, processing, and signing of the senses in the Rite of Acceptance into the Order of Catechumens (RCIA nos. 41ff.); the multiple ceremonies of celebrating God's word, the minor exorcisms, blessings, and anointings during the catechumenate (nos. 81ff.); signing the Book of the Elect during the Rite of Election (nos. 118ff.); the intercessions of the scrutinies and the presentations during the period of purification (nos. 141ff.); and the many moments of water blessing, baptism, anointing, renewal of promises, and sprinkling during the Easter Vigil. These are just a few of the moments that cry out for musical presentation and the ability and gift to weave music artfully through the structure of these rites.

The second issue is that such "ritual music" is not as available from composers and publishers as are hymns and songs. The rites require music that becomes the very language of the rite, not liturgical "filler." The musical forms of acclamations, litanies, and responsorial music need to be developed and implemented in the preparation of these liturgies.

Acclamations, for instance, are more than mere assent; they are statements of investment and commitment, and their place in the RCIA is critical and obvious when one begins to study the rite. Intercessions, litanies, and dialogic musical settings for the presider, cantor, and assembly are needed for the rites of acceptance and election, the scrutinies and the Vigil. These acclamations and litanic forms work best when they are easily memorized by the assembly, needing no verbal directions. Good psalmody is also important, since the word of God (as presented in the lectionary) is at the center of formation and catechesis for the catechumens and candidates throughout their journey, as it is for the whole community.[1] Hymns and songs, while not at the center of these rites, should not be ignored, for they are needed for moments of gathering, procession, anointing, and dismissal. Good musical, liturgical, and pastoral judgments need to govern all decisions in choosing repertoire, with simplicity and accessibility being of highest importance, when we recognize that throughout these rites the primary minister of music is the assembly.

Composers and publishers need to develop more resources for the RCIA. Composers such as Christopher Walker, The Dameans, Tom Conry, Marty Haugen, myself, and others, are beginning to write music specifically for the catechumenate.[2] This is good news, indeed. What follows is a list of musical resources for the various rites of the catechumenate that presents various composers, publishers, and musical styles.[3] No such list can be completely exhaustive, but pastoral musicians should find here some new (and some old) resources to turn to for help and reference for their planning and preparation.

Rite of Acceptance into the Order of Catechumens

ACCLAMATIONS AND RITUAL MUSIC

Acclamations to Respond to the Questioning of the Candidates

We Stand with You. David Haas, GIA (Who Calls You by Name).
I Long for You. Ducote, Daigle, Balhoff, NALR (The Path of Life).
Glory and Praise to You. Lucien Deiss, WLP (Peoples Mass Book—all
  references are to the 1984 edition).

Music for the Procession to the Word

Rejoice in the Lord Always. Christopher Walker, OCP (Music issue).
Those Who Seek Your Face, Lord. Christopher Walker, OCP (Today's
  Missal)
Laudate Dominum. Jacques Berthier, GIA (Music of Taizé, Vol. 1; Wor-
  ship—all references are to the third edition; Gather).
Sing Praises to the Lord. Christopher Walker, OCP (Come to Set Us
  Free).
Gloria III. Jacques Berthier, GIA (Music from Taizé, Vol. 1).
Praise to You, O Christ, Our Savior. Bernadette Farrell, OCP (We Are
  Your People); GIA (Gather).
Let Us Go Rejoicing. Leon C. Roberts, GIA (Mass of St. Paul and Augus-
  tine; Lead Me, Guide Me).
Let Us Go Rejoicing. Michael Joncas, GIA (Gather).
I Rejoiced. John Foley, NALR (Wood Hath Hope; Glory & Praise).
We Walk by Faith. Marty Haugen, GIA (Mass of Creation; Gather);
  NALR (Glory & Praise).
Come, My Children. David Haas, GIA (Who Calls You by Name; Gath-
  er).
Eye Has Not Seen. Marty Haugen, GIA (Gather Us In; Gather); NALR
  (Glory & Praise).

Acclamations for the Signing of the Senses

Lead Me, O Lord (refrain only). Christopher Walker, OCP (Lead Me, O
  Lord).
Eye Has Not Seen (first half of refrain). Marty Haugen, GIA (Gather Us
  In; Gather); NALR (Glory & Praise).
Affirmation of the Assembly/Signing of the Senses/Christ Will Be Your
  Strength. David Haas, GIA (Who Calls You By Name).
May You Receive Christ's Love. Randall DeBruyn, OCP (Today's Mis-
  sal).
Glory and Praise to You. Lucien Deiss, WLP (Peoples Mass Book).

PSALMODY

Psalm 33: Happy the People. Robert E. Kreutz, OCP (Psalms).

Psalm 34: Come, My Children. David Haas, GIA (Who Calls You by Name; Gather).

Psalm 34: Come, My Children. Paul Inwood, OCP.

Psalm 34: Come, My Children. Ducote, Daigle, Balhoff, NALR (Path of Life; Glory & Praise).

Psalm 42: Just Like a Deer. Michael Joncas, NALR (Here in Our Midst).

Psalm 63: I Will Lift Up My Eyes. Tom Conry, OCP (Justice, Like a River); GIA (Gather).

Psalm 63: Your Love Is Finer Than Life. Marty Haugen, GIA (Psalms for the Church Year; Gather).

Psalm 63: My Soul Is Thirsting. Christopher Walker, OCP (Psalms for Feasts and Seasons).

Psalm 63: My Soul Is Thirsting. Niedermeyer, Liturgical Press (Benedictine Book of Song).

Psalm 63: My Soul Is Thirsting. Michael Joncas, GIA (The Winter Name of God; Gather).

HYMNS AND SONGS

Eye Has Not Seen. Marty Haugen, GIA (Gather Us In; Gather); NALR (Glory & Praise).

The Word Is in Your Heart. Bob Hurd (Each Time I Think of You).

We Walk by Faith. Marty Haugen, GIA (Mass of Creation); NALR (Glory & Praise).

Lord of All Hopefulness. Traditional, GIA (Worship).

Lord, I Want to be a Christian. Traditional, spiritual, GIA (Lead Me, Guide Me).

I Have Decided to Follow Jesus. Indian Folk Melody, GIA (Lead Me, Guide Me).

Blessed Are They. David Haas, GIA (To Be Your Bread; Come and Journey; Gather); NALR (Glory & Praise).

Jesus, Come to Us. David Haas, OCP (I Am Yours Today); GIA (Gather).

Rite of Election

ACCLAMATIONS AND RITUAL MUSIC

Lenten Gospel Acclamations

Praise to You, Lord Jesus Christ. Roc O'Connor, NALR (The Steadfast Love).

Praise to You, O Christ, Our Savior. Bernadette Farrell, OCP (We Are Your People); GIA (Gather).

Praise to You, Lord Jesus Christ. David Clark Isele, GIA (Gather to Remember).

Praise to You, Lord Jesus Christ. Christopher Willcock, GIA (ICEL Resource Collection).

Glory to You, O Word of God. David Haas, GIA (Who Calls You by Name).

Praise to You, O Christ. Smith, Geoffrey Chapman (Music for the Mass).

Acclamations and Songs for the Signing of the Book of the Elect

I Have Loved You. Michael Joncas, NALR (On Eagle's Wings; Glory & Praise); GIA (Gather).

Who Calls You by Name. David Haas, GIA (Who Calls You by Name).

Psalm 16: The Center of My Life. Paul Inwood, OCP (Come to Set Us Free).

Psalm 16: Show Us the Path of Life. Marty Haugen, GIA (Mass of Creation).

Psalm 16: The Path of Life. Ducote, Daigle, Balhoff, NALR (The Path of Life; Glory & Praise).

Psalm 16: The Path of Life. David Haas, GIA (Who Calls You by Name).

Lord, You Will Show Us the Path of Life. Moore, GIA (That We May Be One).

Community Blessing. Keyes, Resource Publications (A Gentle Strength).

I Have Called You by Name. Robert M. Hutmacher, GIA..

PSALMODY

Psalm 33: Happy the People. Robert E. Kreutz, OCP (Psalms).

Psalm 51: Be Merciful, O Lord. Marty Haugen, GIA (Psalms for the Church Year; Gather).

Psalm 51: Create in Me a Clean Heart. David Haas, GIA (Light and Peace; Who Calls You by Name; Gather).

Psalm 51: Wash Me with Fresh Water. Robert E. Kreutz, NPM (Psalms for All Seasons).

Psalm 25: Lord, I Give Myself to You. James J. Chepponis, NPM (Psalms for All Seasons).

Psalm 27: The Lord Is My Light. David Haas, GIA (Psalms for the Church Year; Gather); NALR (Glory & Praise).

Psalm 27: The Lord Is My Light. David Haas, GIA (Light and Peace).

Psalm 91: Be with Me. Marty Haugen, GIA (Psalms for the Church Year; Gather); NALR (Glory & Praise).

Psalm 91: Be with Me, Lord. Michael Joncas, OCP (Every Stone Shall Cry).

Psalm 95: Let Us Open Our Lives. Marty Haugen, GIA (Gather Us In).
Psalm 34: Drink in the Richness of God. Howard Hughes, NPM (Psalms for All Seasons).

HYMNS AND SONGS

Come, My Way, My Truth, My Life. R. Vaughan Williams, GIA (Worship).
I Heard the Voice of Jesus Say. Harm. R. Vaughan Williams, GIA (Worship).
Priestly People. Lucien Deiss, WLP (Peoples Mass Book).
I'll Be Somewhere Listening for My Name. Eduardo J. Lango, GIA (Lead Me, Guide Me).
Anthem. Tom Conry, NALR (Ashes; Glory & Praise); GIA (Gather).
Deep Within. David Haas, GIA (As Water to the Thirsty; Who Calls You by Name; Gather).
Church of God. Margaret Daly, GIA (ICEL Resource Collection); NALR (Glory & Praise); OCP (Music Issue).
Tree of Life. Marty Haugen, GIA (Mass of Creation; Gather).
God of Our Journeys. Marty Haugen, GIA (Song of God among Us).
Return to Me. Bob Hurd, OCP (In the Breaking of the Bread); GIA (Gather).
I Have Called You by Name. Robert M. Hutmacher, GIA.
Magnificat. Scottish traditional, Geoffrey Chapman (Music for the Mass).
According to His Plan. Tim Schoenbachler, NALR (O Jerusalem).
We Are Called. David Haas, GIA (Who Calss You by Name; Gather).
I Want to Walk as a Child of the Light. Kathleen Thompson, GIA (Worship).

The Scrutinies

ACCLAMATIONS, INTERCESSIONS, AND RITUAL MUSIC

Jesu Christe Miserere. Jacques Berthier, GIA (Music of Taizé, Vol. 1; Gather).
Kyrie No. 7. Jacques Berthier, GIA (Music of Taizé, Vol. 1; Worship).
Kyrie No. 10. Jacques Berthier, GIA (Music of Taizé, Vol. 1; Worthip; Gather).
Libera Nos, Domine. Jacques Berthier. GIA (Music of Taizé, Vol. 1).
Jesus, Hear Our Prayer. Robert M. Hutmacher, GIA (In Praise of God; Worship).
Litany for Reconciliation. James Hansen, OCP (Litany).

Acclamations for the Scrutinies: God of all power, fountain of grace (1st
Scrutiny); God of all mercy, restore our sight (2nd Scrutiny); God of
the living, not of the dead (3rd Scrutiny). David Haas, GIA (Who Calls
You by Name).
Lord, Have Mercy (from Evening Intercessions). Michael Joncas, NALR
(O Joyful Light).
O Lord, Hear My Prayer. Jacques Berthier, GIA (Music of Taizé, Vol. 2).
O God, Hear Us. Bob Hurd, OCP (In the Breaking of the Bread).
Thuma Mina/Send Me, Jesus. South African, GIA (Gather).
Jesus, Remember Me. Jacques Berthier, GIA (Music of Taizé, Vol. 1;
Worship; Gather).
Adoramus Te, Domine II. Jacques Berthier, GIA (Music of Taizé, Vol. 1;
Worship; Gather).
Jesus, Heal Us. David Haas, GIA (Who Calls You by Name; Gather).
Take the Stone Away, Come Out! Haas/Tufano, GIA (Who Calls You by
Name).
Praise to You, O Christ, Our Savior. Bernadette Farrell, OCP (We Are
Your People); GIA (Gather).
Lord, to Whom Shall We Go? David Haas, GIA (We Have Been Told;
Gather).

PSALMODY

Psalm 51: Be Merciful, O Lord. Marty Haugen, GIA (Psalms for the
Church Year; Gather).
Psalm 51: Be Merciful. Christopher Willcock, OCP (Psalms for Feasts
and Seasons).
Psalm 51: Create in Me a Clean Heart. David Haas, GIA (Light and
Peace; Who Calls You by Name; Gather).
Psalm 51: Give Us, Lord, a New Heart. Bernadette Farrell, OCP (Sing of
the Lord's Goodness).
Psalm 91: Be with Me. Marty Haugen, GIA (Psalms for the Church Year;
Gather).
Psalm 130: With the Lord. Connolly, GIA (We Live a Mystery).
Psalm 130: With the Lord. Michael Joncas, NALR (Here in Our Midst).
Psalm 130: With the Lord There Is Mercy. Marty Haugen, GIA (Psalms
for the Church Year; Gather).
Psalm 130: Out of the Depths. Raffa, Ekklesia Music (Seed, Scattered and
Sown).
Psalm 34: The Cry of the Poor. John Foley, NALR (Wood Hath Hope;
Glory & Praise); GIA (Gather).
Psalm 95: If Today You Hear His Voice. David Haas, GIA (Psalms for
the Church Year; Gather)

Psalm 95: Listen Today to God's Voice. Christopher Willcock, NPM (Psalms for All Seasons).

Psalm 25: Remember Your Mercy, Lord. Paul Inwood, OCP (Sing of the Lord's Goodness); GIA (Gather).

Psalm 25: Remember Your Mercies. David Haas, GIA (To Be Your Bread).

Psalm 23: Shepherd Me, O God. Marty Haugen, GIA (Shepherd Me, O God; Gather).

HYMNS AND SONGS

First Scrutiny: The Woman at the Well

I Heard the Voice of Jesus Say. Harm. R. Vaughan Williams, GIA (Worship).

Come and Let Us Drink of That New River. Kenneth Smith, GIA (Worship).

All Who Drink. James Hansen, OCP (Psalms for Sundays and Seasons).

The Water I Give. David Haas, GIA (Who Calls You by Name; Gather).

Flow, River, Flow. Bob Hurd, OCP (Each Time I Think of You).

Give Us Living Water. Ducote, Daigle, Balhoff, NALR (Path of Life; Glory & Praise).

Living Waters. Suzanne Toolan, GIA (Living Spirit).

Water of Life. David Haas, GIA (As Water to the Thirsty; Who Calls You by Name).

Second Scrutiny: The Man Born Blind

Awake, O Sleeper. Mary Haugen, GIA (Shepherd Me, O God; Gather).

Awake, O Sleeper. Ducote, Daigle, Balhoff, NALR (Path of Life; Glory & Praise).

Awake, You Who Sleep. Huijbers/Oosterhuis, OCP (Vigil; Easter).

Christ Will Be Your Light. David Haas, GIA (Who Calls You by Name).

Awake, O Sleeper, Rise from Death. Tucker/Glaser, GIA (Worship).

Let Us Walk in the Light. Marty Haugen, GIA (Song of God among Us).

God of Our Journeys. Marty Haugen, GIA (Song of God among Us).

Healer of Our Ev'ry Ill. Mary Haugen, GIA (Shepherd Me, O God; Gather).

He Healed the Darkness of My Mind. Haas/Green, GIA (Who Called You by Name).

Amazing Grace. Traditional, GIA (Worship; Lead Me, Guide Me; ICEL Resource Collection); NALR (Glory & Praise); Canadian Catholic Conference—hereafter Canada (Catholic Book of Worship II).

Be Light for Our Eyes. David Haas, GIA (To Be Your Bread; Gather).

Ephphetha. Marty Haugen, GIA (Mass of Creation).

What You Hear in the Dark. Dan Schutte, NALR (Earthen Vessels; Glory & Praise).

Third Scrutiny: The Raising of Lazarus

I am the Resurrection. Ducote, Daigle, Balhoff, NALR (Path of Life).

I Am the Resurrection. David Haas, GIA (Who Calls You by Name; Gather).

I Am the Bread of Life. Suzanne Toolan, GIA (Worship; Gather); NALR (Glory & Praise); Canada (Catholic Book of Worship II).

We Shall Rise Again. Jeremy Young, GIA (Gather).

Unless a Grain of Wheat. Bernadette Farrell, OCP (We Are Your People).

Now We Remain. David Haas, GIA (We Have Been Told; Gather).

We Will Rise Again. David Haas, OCP (Lead Me, O Lord); GIA (Gather).

General Songs for the Scrutinies

God of Day and God of Darkness. Mary Haugen, GIA (Song of God among Us; Come and Journey; Gather).

Be Still. Jeanne Cotter, OCP (Lead Me, O Lord).

There's a Wideness in God's Mercy. Frederick W. Faber, GIA (Worship; ICEL Resource Collection); WLP (Peoples Mass Book).

Hold Us in Your Mercy. Tom Conry, OCP (Justice, Like a River).

There Is a Balm in Gilead. Spiritual, GIA (Worship; ICEL Resource Collection; Lead Me, Guide Me; Gather).

What Wondrous Love Is This. Alexander Means, GIA (Worship; Gather; ICEL Resource Collection); NALR (Glory & Praise); WLP (Peoples Mass Book).

When Jesus Wept. William Billings.

Jesus Walked this Lonesome Valley. American Folk Hymn, GIA (Worship; ICEL Resources Collection); WLP (Peoples Mass Book).

Lord, to Whom Shall We Go? Tom Conry, NALR (We the Living).

Jesus the Lord. Jeffrey Keyes, Resource Publications (A Gentle Strength); GIA (Gather).

We Live a Mystery. Michael Connolly, GIA (We Live a Mystery; Gather).

Remember Your Love. Ducote, Daigle, Balhoff, NALR (Remember Your Love; Glory & Praise); GIA (Gather).

Shelter Me, O God. Bob Hurd, OCP (In the Breaking of the Bread); GIA (Gather).

A Song of Hope. John Foley, NALR (The Steadfast Love).

The Presentation of the Creed

ACCLAMATIONS AND RITUAL MUSIC

Credo I. Jacques Berthier, GIA (Music of Taizé, Vol. 1).
Credo II. Jacques Berthier, GIA (Music of Taizé, Vol. 1).
Credo III. Jacques Berthier, GIA (Music of Taizé, Vol. 2).
I Believe, Lord. Jose Wise, GIA (Songs for the Journey; Gather).
We Believe. David Haas, GIA (Who Calls You by Name).
We Believe. Christopher Walker, OCP (Holy Is God).
We Believe. Jeremy Young, GIA.
The Apostles' Creed. Jacques Berthier, GIA (Worship).
Credimus. Hall, Geoffrey Chapman (Music for the Mass).

PSALMODY

Psalm 19: Lord, You have the Words. David Haas, GIA (Psalms for the Church Year; Gather).
Psalm 19: Lord, You Have the Words. Michael Joncas, OCP (Every Stone Shall Cry).

HYMNS AND SONGS

I Am the Light of the World. Greg Hayakawa, OCP (Roll Down the Ages); GIA (Gather).
We Believe in One True God. Clausnitzer/Lindeman, GIA (ICEL Resource Collection).
Lord, to Whom Shall We Go? Michael Joncas, NALR (On Eagle's Wings).

Presentation of the Lord's Prayer

SETTINGS OF THE LORD'S PRAYER

The Lord's Prayer. Michael Joncas, NALR (Evening Prayer; O Joyful Light; Glory & Praise); GIA (Gather).
The Lord's Prayer I. David Haas, GIA (Morning Praise: Light and Peace; Gather).
Pater Noster. Jacques Berthier, GIA (Music of Taizé, Vol. 1).
The Lord's Prayer. Marty Haugen, GIA (Mass of Creation); NALR (Glory & Praise).
The Lord's Prayer. Alexander Peloquin, GIA (Lyric Liturgy, Worship); Canada (Catholic Book of Worship II).
The Lord's Prayer. David Clark Isele, GIA (Notre Dame Mass).

The Lord's Prayer. Richard Proulx, GIA (A Festival Eucharist; Worship).
The Lord's Prayer. Robert E. Kreutz, OCP (Today's Missal).
The Lord's Prayer. Smith, Geoffrey Chapman (Music for the Mass).
Our Father. Michael Connolly, GIA (We Live a Mystery).
Our Father. Fitzpatrick, Geoffrey Chapman (Music for the Mass).
Our Father. Paul Inwood, Geoffrey Chapman (Music for the Mass).

PSALMODY

Psalm 23: Shepherd Me, O God. Marty Haugen, GIA (Shepherd Me, O God; Gather).
Psalm 23: The Lord Is My Shepherd. Robert E. Kreutz, OCP (Psalms).
Psalm 23: O Christe Domine Jesu. Jacques Berthier, GIA (Music of Taizé, Vol. 2).
Psalm 23: The Lord Is My Shepherd. Joseph Gelineau, GIA (Gelineau Gradual; Worship); Canada (Catholic Book of Worship II).

HYMNS AND SONGS

Because the Lord Is My Shepherd. Chrstopher Walker, OCP (Sing Out the Lord's Goodness); GIA (Gather).
The Living God My Shepherd Is. J. Driscoll, GIA (Worship); Canada (Catholic Book of Worship II).
The King of Love My Shepherd Is. Henry W. Baker, GIA (Worship; ICEL Resource Collection).

Music for Initiation:
Easter Vigil and Easter

ACCLAMATIONS AND RITUAL MUSIC

Acclamations and Ritual Music for the Service of Light

Easter Proclamation. Tom Conry, OCP (Stand).
Blessing of the New Fire, Lumen Christi. Higgins, St. Thomas More Centre (Lord by Your Cross and Resurrection).
Lumen Christi. E. Frese, NPM Publications (Exsultet).
Lumen Christi. Paul Inwood, St. Thomas More Centre (Lord by Your Cross and Resurrection).
Exsultet. Raffa, Ekklesia Music (Seed, Scattered and Sown).
Exsultet. Anslie, St. Thomas More Centre (Lord by Your Cross and Resurrection).
Exsultet, Dialogue Setting. Paul Inwood, St. Thomas More Centre (Lord by Your Cross and Resurrection).

Blessed Are You, Fire of Love. David Haas, GIA (Who Calls You by Name).

The Light of Christ. Marty Haugen, GIA (Octavo ed.).

Glory to God

Glory to God. Jones, OCP (We Are Your People).

Glory to God. David Haas, OCP (As Water to the Thirsty); GIA (Gather).

St. Augustine Gloria. Christopher Walker, OCP (Sing of the Lord's Goodness).

Gloria in Excelsis. Michael Joncas, GIA (The Winter Name of God; Gather).

Glory to God. Michael Joncas, GIA (No Greater Love).

Glory to God, Mass of Creation. Marty Haugen, GIA (Mass of Creation; Gather); NALR (Glory & Praise).

Glory to God, Mass of Remembrance. Marty Haugen, GIA (Shepherd Me, O God; Gather).

Glory to God, Notre Dame Mass. David Clark Isele, GIA (Notre Dame Mass).

Gloria of the Bells. Alexander Peloquin, GIA (Mass of the Bells; Worship).

Litany of the Saints

Jesus, Hear Our Prayer. Robert M. Hutmacher, GIA (In Praise of God).

Litany of the Saints. Grayson Warren Brown, NALR (I Will Rejoice); GIA (Lead Me, Guide Me).

Litany of the Saints. Becker, OCP.

Litany of the Saints. Paul Inwood, St. Thomas More Centre (Lord by Your Cross and Resurrection).

Litany of the Saints. David Haas, GIA (Who Calls You by Name).

Blessing of Water

Blessing of the Water. Richard Proulx, GIA (Worship).

Blessing of the Water. Higgins, St. Thomas More Centre (Lord by Your Cross and Resurrection).

Blessing of the Water. David Haas, GIA (Who Calls You by Name).

Blessed Are You, Water of Life. David Haas, GIA (Who Calls You by Name).

Baptismal Acclamations

All of You Are One. Christopher Willcock, GIA (ICEL Resource Collection).

All of You Are One. David Haas, GIA (Who Calls You by Name).

Blessed Be God, Who Chose You. Arthur Hutchings, GIA (ICEL Resource Collection).

Blessed Be God, Who Chose You. Christopher Willcock, GIA (ICEL Resource Collection).

There Is One Lord. Owen Alstott, OCP (Hymns, Psalms, and Canticles).

There Is One Lord. Lucien Deiss, WLP (Peoples Mass Book).

There Is One Lord. David Haas, GIA (Who Calls You by Name).

There Is One Lord. Jacques Berthier, GIA (Music of Taizé, Vol. 2; Worship).

There Is One Lord. Ducote, Daigle, Balhoff, NALR (Path of Life; Glory & Praise).

There Is One God. Calvin Hampton, GIA (Worship).

Litany of the Holy Spirit. James Hansen, OCP (Litany).

You Are God's Work of Art. Christopher Willcock, GIA (ICEL Resource Collection).

You Are God's Work of Art. David Haas, GIA (Who Calls You by Name; Gather).

You Are God's Work of Art. James Marchionda, WLP (Peoples Mass Book).

Rejoice, You Newly Baptized. Arthur Hutchings, GIA (ICEL Resource Collection).

You Have Put on Christ. Howard Hughes, GIA (Worship; ICEL Resource Collection).

Springs of Water. Kingsley, St. Thomas More Centre (Lord by Your Cross and Resurrection).

Springs of Water. David Haas, GIA (Who Calls You by Name).

God Is Love. Clarence Jos. Rivers, Stimuli, Inc; Canada (Catholic Book of Worship II).

God Is Love. David Haas, GIA (Who Calls You by Name; Gather).

We Believe in You. David Haas, GIA (Who Calls You by Name).

Come to Him and Receive His Light. Russell Woollen, GIA (ICEL Resource Collection).

You Are Called This Day. Carol Dick, PAA (Remember Who We Are).

Holy Church of God, Stretch Out Your Hand. David Haas, GIA (Who Calls You by Name).

Renewal of Baptismal Promises

Renewal of Baptismal Promise. David Haas, GIA (Who Calls You by Name).

We Believe. David Haas, GIA (Who Calls You by Name).

We Believe. Christopher Walker, OCP (Holy Is God).

This Is Our Faith. Arthur Hutchings, GIA (ICEL Resource Collection).

Music for the Sprinkling of Water

Water of Life. David Haas, GIA (As Water to the Thirsty; Who Calls You by Name).

Song of Fire and Water. Marty Haugen, GIA (Mass of Creation); NALR (Glory & Praise).

Song over the Waters. Marty Haugen, GIA (Shepherd Me, O God; Gather).

God, Our Fountain of Salvation. Christopher Walker, OCP.

Cleanse Us, O Lord. Michael Joncas, GIA (God of Life and of the Living).

Song of the Chosen. Rory Cooney, NALR (Do Not Fear to Hope).

Water of Life. Stephen Dean, OCP (Come to Set Us Free).

Jubilate Deo. Jacques Berthier, GIA (Music of Taizé, Vol. 1; Worship; Gather).

Flow, River, Flow. Bob Hurd, OCP (Each Time I Think of You).

I Saw the Living Water. Lucien Deiss, NALR (Glory & Praise).

There Is One Lord. Owen Alstott, OCP (Psalms, Hymns, and Canticles).

All Creatures of Our God and King. Francis of Assisi, GIA (Worship); WLP (Peoples Mass Book); Canada (Catholic Book of Worship II).

Awake, O Sleeper, Rise from Death. F. Bland Tucker, GIA (Worship).

Grant to Us, O Lord. Lucien Deiss, WLP (Peoples Mass Book).

There Is a River. Tim Manion, NALR (There Is a River; Glory & Praise).

Music for Communion

Now in This Banquet. Marty Haugen, GIA (Song of God among Us; Gather).

Now We Remain. David Haas, GIA (We Have Been Told; Gather).

You Are Our Living Bread. Michael Joncas, NALR (Here in Our Midst; Glory & Praise).

We Remember. Marty Haugen, GIA (With Open Hands; Gather); NALR (Glory & Praise).

Seed, Scattered and Sown. Dan Feiten, Ekklesia Music (Seed, Scattered and Sown); GIA (Gather).

Taste and See. Michael Connolly, GIA (We Live a Mystery).

Taste and See. Christopher Walker, OCP (Come to Set Us Free).

Taste and See. Marty Haugen, GIA (Psalms for the Church Year; Gather).

Taste and See. James Moore, GIA (Gather); NALR (Glory & Praise).

Taste and See. Dean, OCP (We Are Your People).

Eat This Bread. Jacques Berthier, GIA (Music of Taizé, Vol. 2; Worship; Gather).

Lord, We Share in This One, True Bread. Christopher Walker, OCP (Sing of the Lord's Goodness).

As Grain Once Scattered. Tom Conry, OCP (Stand).

In the Breaking of the Bread. Bob Hurd, OCP (In the Breaking of the Bread); GIA (Gather).

Life-Giving Bread, Saving Cup. James Chepponis, GIA (Gather).

Blessing Prayer. David Haas, GIA (Who Calls You by Name).

Jesus, the Bread of Life. Grayson Warren Brown, GIA (Lead Me, Guide Me); NALR (Glory & Praise).

Psalmody and Music for the Word

Psalm 104: Lord, Send Out Your Spirit. Paul Lisicky, GIA (Cantor/Congregation Series; Gather).

Psalm 104: Lord, Send Out Your Spirit. Tim Schoenbachler, OCP (All Is Ready).

Psalm 104: Lord, Breathe Your Spirit. Krisman/Hughes, NPM (Psalms for All Seasons).

Psalm 104: Lord, Send Out Your Spirit. David Haas, GIA (Psalms for the Church Year).

Psalm 104: Lord, Send Out Your Spirit. Alexander Peloquin, GIA (Songs of Israel).

Psalm 104: Lord, Send Out Your Spirit. David Clark Isele, GIA (Psalms for the Church Year).

Psalm 104. Tony Barr, St. Thomas More Centre (Lord by Your Cross and Resurrection).

Psalm 16: Preserve Me, Lord. Christopher Walker, OCP (Lead Me, O Lord).

Psalm 16. Bill Tamblyn, St. Thomas More Centre (Lord by Your Cross and Resurrection).

Canticle of Moses. Tony Barr, St. Thomas More Centre (Lord by Your Cross and Resurrection).

The Baptismal Memorial. Howard Hughes, GIA (Praise God in Song).

I Will Sing to My God. Marty Haughen, GIA (Psalms for the Church Year, Vol. 2).

Psalm 30: I Will Praise You, Lord. Paul Inwood, OCP (Come to Set Us Free); GIA (Gather).

You Will Draw Water. Tom Conry, NALR (We the Living); GIA (Gather).

Psalm 19: Lord, You Have the Words. Michael Joncas, OCP (Every Stone Shall Cry).

Psalm 19: Lord, You Have the Words. David Haas, GIA (Psalms for the Church Year; Gather).

Psalm 42: Just Like a Deer. Michael Joncas, NALR (Here in Our Midst).

Psalm 51: Create in Me a Clean Heart. David Haas, GIA (Light and Peace; Who Calls You by Name; Gather).

Psalm 136: His Love Is Everlasting. Haas/Haugen, GIA (Psalms for the Church Year).

Psalm 136: Give Thanks to the Lord. Joseph Gelineau, GIA (The Gelineau Gradual).

Psalm 136: Your Love Is Never Ending. Marty Haugen, GIA (Shepherd Me, O God; Gather).

Psalm 136: Eternal Is His Mercy. Michael Joncas, NALR (On Eagle's Wings).

Psalm 118: This Is the Day. Robert E. Kreutz, OCP (Psalms).

Psalm 118: This Is the Day. Michael Joncas, OCP (Every Stone Shall Cry).

Psalm 118: Christus Resurrexit. Jacques Berthier, GIA (Music of Taizé, Vol. 2); Worship).

Psalm 118: Let Us Rejoice. Marty Haugen, GIA (Psalms for the Church Year; Gather).

Psalm 118: Now Comes the Day. Tom Conry, OCP (Stand).

Psalm 118: This Is the Day. Christopher Willcock, OCP (Psalms for Feasts and Seasons).

Psalm 118: This Is the Day. David Clark Isele, GIA (Psalms for Feasts and Seasons).

The Story of Creation. Tom Conry, OCP (Vigil: Easter).

God Spoke to Our Father Abraham. Connaughton/Schiavone, GIA (Worship).

Isaiah 55 (Sung Reading). St. Thomas More Centre (Lord by Your Cross and Resurrection).

When Israel Was in Egypt's Land (Let My People Go). Spiritual, GIA (Worship; Lead Me, Guide Me).

When Israel Made Her Way from Egypt. Huijbers/Oosterhuis, OCP (Vigil: Easter).

All Who Are Thirsty. Michael Connolly, GIA (We Live a Mystery).

Come to the Water. John Foley, NALR (Wood Hath Hope; Glory & Praise); GIA (Gather).

Easter Alleluia. Marty Haugen, GIA (Song of God among Us; Gather).

Easter Alleluia. Michael Joncas, GIA (God of Life and of the Living).

Praise His Name. Michael Joncas, NALR (On Eagle's Wings); GIA (Gather).

Celtic Alleluia. Walker/O'Carroll, OCP (Sing of the Lord's Goodness).

Alleluia! Let Us Rejoice. David Haas, GIA (Light and Peace; Who Calls You by Name).

Alleluia. Ducote, Daigle, Balhoff, NALR (Path of Life; Glory & Praise).

Joyful Alleluia. Howard Hughes, GIA (Cantor/Congregation Series).

Alleluia, Sing! David Haas, GIA (To Be Your Bread; Gather).

Alleluia! Speak, O Lord. Marty Haugen, GIA (Shepherd Me, O God).

Sing Praises to the Lord. Christopher Walker, OCP (Come to Set Us Free).

Up from the Earth. Rory Cooney, NALR (Mystery).

Why Do You Look? Tom Conry, OCP (Vigil: Easter).

Psallite Deo. Jacques Berthier, GIA (Music of Taizé, Vol. 2; Gather).

Surrexit Christus. Jacques Berthier, GIA (Music of Taizé, Vol. 2; Gather).

The Earth Is Full. Dan Feritan, Ekklesia Music (Seed, Scattered and Sown).

God Is Alive! David Haas, GIA (Light and Peace; Who Calls You by Name; Gather).

Hymn of Initiation. Kreutz/Westendorf, NALR (Glory & Praise).

Praised Be the Father. Ducote, Daigle, Balhoff, NALR (Path of Life; Glory & Praise).

At the Lamb's High Feast We Sing. Robert Campbell, GIA (Worship; ICEL Resource Collection); Canada (Catholic Book of Worship II).

Baptized in Water. Michael A. Saward, GIA (Worship; Gather).

Festival Canticle: Worthy Is Christ (This Is the Feast). Richard Hillert, GIA (Worship).

Song of the Risen One. David Haas, GIA (Who Calls You by His Name; Gather).

Awake, You Who Sleep. Huijbers/Oosterhuis, OCP (Vigil: Easter).

I Will Not Die. Tom Conry, OCP (Justice, Like a River); GIA (Gather).

Canticle of the Sun. Marty Haugen, GIA (With Open Hands; Gather); NALR (Glory & Praise).

All Shall Be Well. John Foley, NALR (The Steadfast Love; Glory & Praise).

Hail Thee, Festival Day. R. Vaughan Williams, GIA (Worship); WLP (Peoples Mass Book); Canada (Catholic Book of Worship II).

Now the Green Blade Rises. John Crum, GIA (Worship); WLP (Peoples Mass Book); Canada (Catholic Book of Worship II).

Surrexit Dominus Vere II. Jacques Berthier, GIA (Music of Taizé, Vol. 1; Gather).

Paschal Procession. Christopher Walker, OCP (We Are Your People).

Shout for Joy. Spiritual, arr. Smith, Geoffrey Chapman (Music for the Mass).

Mystagogia and Mission

Let Us Walk in the Light. Marty Haugen, GIA (Gather to Remember).

In Christ There Is No East or West. John Oxenham/Spiritual, GIA (Worship; Lead Me, Guide Me); NALR (Glory & Praise); WLP (Peoples Mass Book); Canada (Catholic Book of Worship II).

The Servant Song. Richard Gillard, Fisherfolk (Cry Hosanna); GIA (Gather).

Bring Forth the Kingdom. Marty Haugen, GIA (Song of God among Us; Gather).

They Who Do Justice. Bob Hurd, OCP (In the Breaking of the Bread).

Anthem. Tom Conry, NALR (Ashes; Glory & Praise); GIA (Gather).

Blest Are They. David Haas, GIA (To Be Your Bread; Come and Journey; Gather); NALR (Glory & Praise).

Sing of the Lord's Goodness. Ernest Sands, OCP (Sing of the Lord's Goodness); GIA (Gather).

Jubilate Deo. Jacques Berthier, GIA (Music of Taizé, Vol. 1; Worship; Gather).

Glorious in Majesty. Jeff Cothran, GIA (Worship; Gather).

He Has Anointed Me. Ducote, Daigle, Balhoff, NALR (Path of Life; Glory & Praise); GIA (Gather).

Come Down, O Love Divine. Bianco da Siena/Vaughan Williams, GIA (Worship); WLP (Peoples Mass Book); Canada (Catholic Book of Worship II).

Send Us Your Spirit. David Haas, GIA (To Be Your Bread; Gather).

On Our Journey to the Kingdom. Tobias Colgan, OCP (Today's Missal).

Sing Out, Earth and Skies. Marty Haugen, GIA (Song of God among Us; Gather).

We Are Many Parts. Marty Haugen, GIA (With Open Hands; Gather).

We Are Called. David Haas, GIA (Who Calls You by Name; Gather).

The Kingdom of God on the Way. Tom Conry, NALR (We the Living).

When You Call. Carol Dick, PAA (Remember Who We Are).

The Harvest of Justice. David Haas, GIA (To Be Your Bread; Gather).

Jesus Still Lives. Suzanne Toolan, WLP (Renew Us, Lord); GIA (Gather).

Keep Each Other. Carol Dick, PAA (Remember Who We Are).

God of All Creation. David Haas, GIA (As Water to the Thirsty; Gather).

Spirit of God within Me. Joncas/Dudley-Smith, GIA (Come and Journey; Gather).

Send Us Your Spirit. Dan Schutte, NALR (The Steadfast Love; Glory & Praise).

Go Out to the World. Ron Krisman, GIA (Cantor/Congregation Series).

Go Out to the World. Michael Joncas, NALR (On Eagle's Wings).

Go Out to the Whole World (Round). Tamblyn, Geoffrey Chapman (Music for the Mass).

You Are the Voice. David Haas, GIA (We Have Been Told; Gather); NALR (Glory & Praise).

A New Song. James E. Moore, Jr., GIA (That We May Be One; Gather).

Still Must We Walk. Tom Conry, OCP (Stand).

There Is a River. Tim Manion, NALR (There Is a River; Glory & Praise).

Shepherd of Our Hearts. James Chepponis, GIA.

That We May Be One. James E. Moore, Jr., GIA (That We May Be One).

Let the People Say. Tim Manion, NALR (There Is a River; Glory & Praise).

Soon and Very Soon. A. Crouch, GIA (Lead Me, Guide Me).

Lord, You Gave the Great Commission. Jeffrey Rowthorn, GIA (Worship).

Go, Make of All Disciples. Leon M. Adkins, GIA (Worship).

Be Light for Our Eyes. David Haas, GIA (To Be Your Bread; Gather).

Song of St. Patrick. Marty Haugen, GIA (Song of God among Us; Gather).

Veni, Sancte Spiritus. Jacques Berthier, GIA (Music of Taizé, Vol. 1; Worship; Gather).

I Will Be With You. James E. Moore, Jr., GIA (Gather).

Happy Are They Who Believe. David Haas, GIA (As Water to the Thirsty).

Spirit of God. Marty Haugen, GIA (Shepherd Me, O God).

Notes

1. The psalms are being rediscovered as important resources for worship, and new settings are being written all the time, especially with new, inclusive texts. Parishes that presently use the psalms in worship can find parallels to the settings included in this list from older resources, such as the Gelineau settings of the Grail translation and the settings found in the *Peoples Mass Book*.

2. This is not to say that other music cannot be adapted to the stages of the catechumenate. Many parishes have been doing this with available repertoire already, and some of the hymns, psalms, and acclamations that have been available are included in this list. But I am looking at music written with the catechumenate in mind and, for the most part, now available in more accessible formats, such as new hymnals.

3. [Editor's Note] One resource that we became aware of too late to include in this list is the new collection of music and other resources for the RCIA provided by Cooperative Ministries. Titled *Reborn to Life*, it contains music by some of the composers listed here (Michael Joncas, Christopher Willcock, Tim Schoenbachler), new music by other composers, and selected articles and supplemental resources. For further information write: Cooperative Ministries, Inc., PO Box 4463, Washington DC 20017-4463. (800) 999-7729.

Publishers

Canadian Conference of Catholic
  Bishops
Publications Service
90 Parent Avenue
Ottawa, Ontario
Canada K1N 7B1

Ekklesia Music, Inc.
PO Box 22967
Denver CO 80222

Fisherfolk
Hope Publishing Co.
380 S. Main Street
Carol Stream IL 60187

Geoffrey Chapman
Cassell Ltd.
1 Vincent Square
London, SW1P 2PN
Great Britain

GIA Publications, Inc.
7404 South Mason Avenue
Chicago IL 60638

Liturgical Press
Collegeville MN 56321

North American Liturgy Resources
  (NALR)
10802 N. 23rd Avenue
Phoenix AZ 85029

NPM Publications
225 Sheridan St. NW
Washington, DC 20011

Oregon Catholic Press
  (OCP)
5536 NE Hassalo
Portland OR 97213

Pastoral Arts Associates
  (PAA)
642 N. Grandview Avenue
Daytona Beach FL 32018

Resource Publications
160 E. Virginia St. #290
San Jose CA 95112

St. Thomas More Centre
9/11 Henry Road
London, N4 2LH
Great Britain

Stimuli, Inc.
Box 20066
Cincinnati OH 45220

World Library Publications
  (WLP)
3815 N. Willow Road
Schiller Park IL 60176

THIRTEEN

MUSIC FOR THE THREE DAYS

I remember sporting my new dress shoes while walking proudly the half-mile to St. Casimir Church in spring 1956. Choosing a new pair of shoes each year was no casual affair; I scoured catalogues and newspaper ads carefully to select the latest style that would give me the fit and feel of being "cool." These shoes could only be worn somewhere special, like church or grandma's. This ritual of search and selection coincided each year with Holy Week, which meant vacation, which meant lots of time in church. And in this particular year there seemed to be a rising demand for altar boys and extra practices with Father for some new, complicated way of doing Mass.

Even though I was a novice, I somehow managed to be chosen to crew the "big" Holy Week events, no doubt due to a proclivity for parroting Latin and a knack for stage directions. I can still amost see my penciled-in blocking in my first "New Holy Week" booklet (a precursor of the missalette), the one with the paschal lamb logo on the cover. To this third grade server, the seemingly monumental task of learning the new rubrics gave a feeling of awe and terror, just when I was becoming comfortable with the rigors of the regular "low" and "high" Mass routine.

Living Participation

Five months before Holy Week that spring, the decree *Maxima Redemptionis* had been issued by the Sacred Congregation of Rites. It was meant, its authors suggested, to offer the church a "living participation" in the culmination of the liturgical year. Its reforms confirmed the 1951 experimental restoration of the Easter Vigil, simplified the rites, and returned to the earlier practice of a single evening and afternoon liturgies for Holy Thursday and Good Friday, so that the whole church could "re-live the great central mystery of redemption with greater conscious, active and devout participation." This renewal was successfully implemented in parishes where the decree's stress on catechesis to understand the "liturgical meaning and pastoral purpose of the rubrics" was taken seriously. Special booklets of "Masses of Holy Week and the Easter Vigil" were in high demand; one publisher sold over a million copies that first year. A report on the New Holy Week in *America* (April 21, 1956) showed glowing support for the solemn rites and indications that people participated as never before:

> Participated they did . . . they came in vast numbers despite weather sometimes adverse. They eagerly entered upon every part assigned to them. They were profoundly awed and moved as the solemnities unfolded in their midst. Afterward they spoke of the entire experience with enthusiasm. It struck home to their souls.

This was a dramatic challenge to the average Catholic, whose previous celebration of Holy Week had consisted of Palm Sunday, the stations of the cross on Friday, Easter egg dyeing on Saturday, and Easter Day itself.

For the under-forty crowd or those whose memories might blur a bit, the rituals' musical *ordo de rigeur* can be found in the pre-Vatican II Roman Missal or in *The Rites of Holy Week*, Chapter Four, "Rules for Music."[1] Musical instructions for the celebrant, choir, and congregation were explicit. For the people, singing in these rites did not represent a radical departure from the normative Sunday milieu. Latin was the language, and minimal congregational responses at high Mass were familiar. In some parishes, especially at school Masses, sung chant ordinarily thrived along with a limited repertoire of devotional and national hymns. Musical leadership was to be found in enthusiastic choirs reveling in neo-polyphonic Caecilianism and a staple, traditional repertoire from the familiar *St. Gregory*, the *Pius X*, or the *St. Basil* hymnals.

The people's part in the singing consisted primarily in basic, fixed chants, and particular music became associated with certain events. *Ubi caritas* accompanied the foot washing (the *Mandatum*, if indeed it took place), and the *Pange, Lingua* became the processional for transferring the Blessed Sacrament on Holy Thursday. The "Mass of the Presanctified" on Good Friday was marked by the Passion and collect chants (*Flectamus genua . . . Levate*), the chants during the adoration of the cross (*Popule meus* and *Venite, adoremus*), and cues from a wooden clapper. *Lumen Christi!*: a cry in the dark heralded the Easter Vigil in all its protracted glory, with the *Exsultet*, the ringing of bells, the litany of the saints, and the sometimes wavering triple Easter Alleluia. Easter Day began with the sprinkling of water accompanied by the *Vidi aquam* and moved to the sequence *Victimae paschali*.

Music to Express the Mystery

With the renewed post-Vatican II liturgy, many of the sounds we had come to associate with the Holy Week rituals seemed inadequate to express the mystery at the heart of the paschal cycle. With some exceptions (the *Pange Lingua*, the *Exsultet*, the litany of the saints, and the Easter Alleluia), most chant was eliminated or replaced with adaptations in English.

Furthermore, the flicker of participation ignited a decade before had begun an inevitable blaze toward new composition and a discovery of the hymn tradition. Many of the earliest hymns chosen for use during the triduum favored texts that historicized these liturgies: "At That First Eucharist," "When I Behold the Wondrous Cross," "O Come and Mourn," "Were You There," "Jesus Christ Is Risen Today," and "Ye Sons and Daughters." The words "commemoration," "re-enactment," and "re-living," which were part of the theology for the initial recovery of Holy Week, began to find expression in new music that similarly gave a historicized shape to the meaning of the triduum. With the use of the vernacular and with a somewhat diminished sense of mystery and symbol, that music seemed to convey a sense of Holy Week as a trip on the "Bible Land Mystery Bus Tour."[2]

From the recovery of the rites in the 1950s to today's evolution of the triduum, music has shaped our celebrations and altered our understanding of the triduum event. The General Norms for the Liturgical Year (1969) instill a unity and singular focus to the three days that transcend past cultural and ecclesial traditions of historical representation.[3] Any reference to distinct passion/death events occurring on three distinct days (Thursday, Friday, and Saturday), with the assignment of a separate cause for celebration on Easter Sunday, has to come to grips with the term *pascha*, which the new calendar uses to denote the passion *as well* as the resurrection.[4] Because of the more fluid musical environment to which we have moved since the 1950s, our choices can affect the meaning of the rite. For instance, one practice that could enhance the unity of *pascha* would be the use of one piece of music that could accompany a different rite each day: the foot washing, the veneration of the cross, and the communion rite.

Singing beyond the Surface

In recent years parishes have moved beyond the surface of the paschal events to singing about their significance and their social implications. We are gradually becoming aware that we cannot rejoice in the rising of Jesus without first sharing in the dying experience of others.

One important question to ask before choosing the music and texts for the triduum is: How do we focus ritually on Jesus Christ? Are we singing about Jesus' (historical) death, or are we celebrating Christ's dying today? It takes a far different commitment to sing about the Christ Jesus of faith than the Jesus of history.

The question poses some serious challenges to our conceptions of Holy Week. For instance, does Holy Thursday solemnize the doctrine of transubstantiation and the institution of the ministerial priesthood, or is it a time for the entire *parish* to celebrate and renew its commitment to ministry? If this liturgy is a parish commitment to ministry, the foot washing (and not some euphemistic substitute) becomes a significant symbolic act—deeper than a sign of humility—and it is shaped by the texts sung while it takes place. A parish might choose, then, to sing Richard Gillard's "The Servant Song":

Will you let me be your servant,
Let me be as Christ to you;
Pray that I may have the grace
to let you be my servant too.[5]

Other possibilities to express similar meaning would include the Ghana folk song translated by Tom Colvin, "Jesu, Jesu," and Jeffery Rowthorn's beautiful text, "Lord, You Give the Great Commission."[6]

Good Friday's passion narrative might take on a whole new character if, instead of playing the familiar role of the "crowd," the assembly joins in singing acclamations of faith or stanzas of a hymn at selected places during the proclamation. Christopher Walker's "Passion Acclamation" would serve nicely: "Jesus has given his life for us!"[7] Other possibilities include Willard Jabusch's "When We Think How Jesus Suffered" and Alexander Means' and Marty Haugen's "Good Friday Hymn," sung to the American tune *Wondrous Love*:

As you have shown the way, let us love, let us love . . .
As you have shown the way, so teach us every day
To simply be the way of your love, of your love . . . [8]

And here are a few examples of music for the Easter Vigil and Easter Day that communicate strong interrelationships between the totality of worship and life: Christopher Walker's "Paschal Procession," Bernard Huijbers' "Maybe, Now and Then," Fortunatus' sixth century *Salva festa dies* translated and set to R. Vaughan Williams' tune as "Hail Thee, Festival Day," and Brian Wren's "Christ Is Alive."

Herald of the Future

Music is usually thought of as reflecting the dynamic of a social system. But Jacques Attali, a French economist and philosopher, makes a case for music as a proactive element, foreshadowing trends that shape society. Whether he is tracing the economic climate of the nineteenth century to influences from eighteenth century classicism, or tracing the political activism of the 1960s to the radical folk tone in the music of Bob Dylan and his comrades, Attali sees music and sound as heralding new meaning, new ritual, and new communication. Similarly, music has the potential to foreshadow, shape, and express the future of liturgical rites and their meaning. In this capacity our song becomes "not only the image of things but the transcending of the everyday—the herald of the future. It makes audible a new world that will gradually become visible."[9]

No amount of theorizing or catechizing on the RCIA can create the kind of prophetic influence that music can have on the rite and the community. The implications of that fact for the triduum are enormous, beyond the reach of our imaginations at present. Let's hope that David Haas' collection *Who Calls You by Name: Music for Christian Initiation* is a harbinger of the kind of synergy needed to keep our rituals from becoming frozen, meaningless voids.

We are now beginning to discover that the rites do not dictate the use of music that celebrates the past. Instead, our music has a voice in shaping our rituals and thus our spirituality. Claiming our past is an important step toward creating our future, but a thoughtless reliance on texts that try to place us in the upper room, at the foot of the cross, or in the tomb can be a disservice to the real meaning of the paschal rites. Equally tempting to empty illusion is ritual music that creates an aesthetic atmosphere for its own sake, filling time, responding for the sake of response. We don't need music for the triduum that celebrates a church mimicking, representing, or repeating itself; we need compositions that nourish a faith inspiring us to re-create, serve, and live.

Notes

1. Frederick R. McManus, *The Rites of Holy Week* (Paterson, NJ: St. Anthony Guild Press, 1956).

2. Samuel Torvend, O.P., *Threshing Floor* (Archdiocese of St. Paul and Minneapolis) 6:3 (January 1989).

3. See Patrick Regan, "The Three Days and the Forty Days," *Worship* 53:1 (January 1980) 2–18.

4. See *The Roman Calendar: Text and Commentary* (Washington, DC: United States Catholic Conference, 1976).

5. Richard Gillard, "The Servant Song," *Cry Hosanna* and *Gather* (Chicago, IL: GIA Publications, Inc., 1988).

6. Tom Colvin, "Jesu, Jesu" (Carol Stream, IL: Hope Publishing Co., 1982), in *Worship* and *Gather* (GIA); Jeffery Towthorn, "Lord, You Give the Great Commission" (text copyright Jeffery W. Rowthorn, 1978; music from Hope Publishing Co., Carol Strean, IL, 1970) in *Worship* (GIA). Both are also in *The Hymnal 1982* (New York: Church Hymnal Corporation, 1987).

7. Christopher Walker, "Passion Acclamation," in *Today's Missal*(Portland, OR: Oregon Catholic Press, 1989).

8. Willard F. Jabusch, "When We Think How Jesus Suffered," in the *Peoples Mass Book* (Schiller Park, IL: World Library Publications, 1984); Alexander Means (st. 1) and Marty Haugen (st. 2–5), "Good Friday Hymn," in *Gather* (GIA, 1988).

9. Jacques Attali, *Noise: The Political Economy of Music*, trans. Brian Massimi (Minneapolis, MN: University of Minnesota Press, 1985).

FOURTEEN

INITIATION AT EASTER: CHALLENGING THE MUSICIAN

The Rite of Christian Initiation of Adults, even in its revised form, offers a challenge to liturgy planners and musicians in preparing the already complex and sometimes cluttered celebration of the Vigil of Easter. This brief essay will address two concerns: how the initiatory rites fit into the larger structure of the Easter Vigil as presented in the Roman Missal, and how music functions in the initiatory rites.

The United States edition of the RCIA outlines the initiatory rites at the Vigil in several sections of the text. The first outline (nos. 206–243) presents the rites of initiation when only the elect are to be initiated. Appendix I-4 (nos. 562–594) presents the rites when the elect and the candidates for full communion join in the same celebration. A third outline, to be used only when children of catechetical age are to be initiated, is in the first section of Part II (nos. 304–329).[1]

The Paschal Context

All of these initiatory outlines assume as the context of initiation the complexus of rite, word, and song that make up the Easter Vigil, proximately, and the triduum, which allows the Vigil to speak within the larger paschal memory, remotely. The RCIA offers little to assist parish ministers in making this vital connection of context, and, therefore, parish ministers would be wise to seek out other sources that could assist them in doing so.[2]

Three points need to be mentioned here in regard to the Vigil as context for the initiatory rites.

1. The proclamation of the word during the Easter Vigil is the fertile ground from which Christian initiation takes shape and meaning. Careful attention must be paid to the verbal and nonverbal texts uttered in the assembly. Verbal texts include the readings from the lectionary, the blessing prayers of fire, water, bread, and wine, the orations, hymnody, responses, and the homily. Nonverbal texts include the construction and placement of the ambo, the font, the paschal candle, and the table, the positioning of the elect and the candidates, as well as other environmental considerations of festivity.

Attention to the details through which these texts are proclaimed allows the possibility for the meaning of initiation to be grounded in the vision of God's reign, which resounds with shining splendor in the night, shatters the fetters of Egypt, and alone gives authenticity to the gathering.

2. While the initiation rites only begin after the homily at the Vigil, the integration of initiatory imagery into the liturgy should begin long before and continue for the remainder of the celebration. The orations after the readings, for instance, offer the presider the option of praying for those to be initiated. Creative liturgy planners and musicians could also create other texts for song or blessing that would mention those to be initiated either explicitly or by innuendo. What is important, it seems, is a consistent orientation given to the Vigil, so that its many images and symbols harmonize, rather than appearing to be so many random pieces that appear haphazardly, without direction.

Musicians would do well to think in terms of a leitmotif, that is, a recurrent musical subject that could be used throughout the Vigil or perhaps the entire triduum. Employing this musical genre links the celebrations with a common sound and symbol. For example, the ancient text *Christus factus est pro nobis obediens . . .* from the *Liber Usualis* could be set to music in an English translation and sung at various moments throughout the triduum or the Vigil. These moments could include the music during the washing of feet, the eucharistic prayer on Holy Thursday, during the liturgy of the hours, at the veneration of the cross or the communion service on Good Friday, and at various times during the Vigil.[3]

CHALLENGING THE MUSICIAN 139

Other texts that speak of the work of Christ as conqueror of the underworld, whose blood we plead before the face of God, could ground the initiation rites in a Christology that views being in Christ as the goal of all conversion and initiation.

3. It is important for musicians and liturgy planners to be conscious that the apex of the initiatory rites is eating and drinking at the eucharistic celebration. Because of the importance of the water bath, the explanatory rites, and the chrismation, the eucharistic prayer and the breaking of bread and sharing of the cup are often treated as an afterthought at the Vigil. The initiatory rites are often fashioned to make immersion (which, if we are not careful, can become an amusing middle-class pastime of a public bath in a rented spa) both the central focus of the Vigil and its climax. It is not.

While it is true that these rites are a once-in-a-lifetime event, the context of the initiatory rites is the proclamation of the pasch of Christ, which finds its fullest meaning in the great prayer of the eucharist and in the eating and drinking that the neophytes do— wet, oily, dazed, and in awe as they are—with the community for the first time that night. Liturgists and musicians need to be conscious of this issue and seek ways to show that the gathering around the bread and cup are the zenith of the paschal night.

Music for the Initiatory Rites

When Christians gather at the full moon of the spring equinox, they truly have something to sing about. The great night celebrates the cosmic renewal that directs history afresh in the memory of Christ. Such a night regenerates the community in the covenant that God has made with the people. It is the night of awakening to the world that lies beyond death, in which, even now, the community lives in hope. This night of paschal memory is given a significant twist when, in the midst of jubilee, new members are initiated.

We need to look at the musical questions raised when the initiatory rites complete the paschal memory. What music is specifically *necessary* for the initiation rites at the Vigil? How does the music selected for the initiation rites influence the selection of music for the rest of the Vigil? When a parish uses the combined rites of initiation at the Vigil, initiating the unbaptized and receiving baptized people into full communion, how does music for that event differ from music for initiating the unbaptized only, or from music for a Vigil in which no one is baptized, but people are received into full communion and confirmed? Each of these events needs a few comments, which may invite further thinking about them.

1. *Required Music for Initiation.* When initiation of the unbaptized is celebrated at the Vigil, the following musical moments are prescribed in the RCIA: the litany of the saints, the blessing of the waters with the acclamation of the assembly, the assembly's acclamation-response to the baptism, the song between baptism and confirmation, and the song during the sprinkling of the assembly with the baptismal water.

With the exception of the songs between baptism and confirmation and during the sprinkling with baptismal water, these prescribed moments are all acclamatory responses that bring the assembly into the ritual initiatory activity. With the help of a competent cantor and choir, the assembly can be brought into places it has never been before: the procession to the font, the water blessing, and the bath. Simple, well-crafted acclamations, with texts that move the ritual along, are well suited to these moments. Sample texts for hymns and acclamations from biblical and liturgical sources (found in the RCIA, Appendix II, nos. 595–597) are begging to be set to music; they would serve the initiatory rites and the assembly's participation well.[4] Some of these acclamations, as suggested above, could serve as a leitmotif to be brought forward again, during the eucharistic prayer or at other moments in the Vigil. There is no need to be too fancy; keep the music simple and singable, so that the assembly will need no music participation aid, keeping their hands free for applause, touch, and prayer.

2. *Music for the Rest of the Vigil.* When the parish is initiating new members, should the music for the whole Vigil be different than at Vigils when there is no initiation? Should the initiatory rites influence the other musical choices for this occasion? The author thinks no and yes. No, in that the music for the Vigil, whether there are initiatory rites or not, should sing the festivity of the occasion and the paschal memory that the church is keeping. Yes, in that the importance of maintaining the orientation of initiation would call for an integration of texts and song, like the

leitmotif suggested above, to keep the litany well focused and connected.

One pastoral consideration when there are initiatory rites at the Vigil, however, is that the choice of music should allow the new members to participate. In other words, musicians should choose, teach, and integrate into the Vigil music that would be familiar to the elect and the candidates, to allow their sung participation in the rituals of the entire night. The music could have been chosen well in advance and incorporated into the catechetical and liturgical sessions with the elect during the period of purification.

3. *Music for combined ceremonies.* Our last concern is whether there should be a musical difference between a parish's celebration of a combined ritual of initiation/reception at the Vigil and its celebration of initiation alone or reception into full communion alone.

In the combined rites of Appendix I of the RCIA, the added difference when the rites are combined is "The Reception" (nos. 584–586). It consists of the invitation to the candidates to come to the table, a profession of faith, and the act of reception.[5] No musical response or acclamation is noted. The combined rites continue with confirmation (nos. 587ff), in which the candidates and neophytes participate together. So it seems that the combined rites ask no more musically than the initiatory rites described in other sections of the RCIA. Yet pastoral sense might add an acclamation to the reception rite as a musical support to and approval of the ritual activity.[6]

Some additional music may be needed, however, if immersion is the parish's baptismal practice. There is ample time for a hymn while the neophytes change their apparel and come forward dressed in their white garments. A hymn of praise, a song invoking the Spirit, the Gloria, or another Easter hymn could be used. The hymn would draw to a close when the neophytes enter the assembly, the rite of reception would be celebrated, and the entire group of neophytes and candidates would be sealed in confirmation. An ostinato during the entire confirmation could support the action of chrismation.

The initiation rites should be done simply and well. They point ultimately to the proclamation of the paschal memorial at the table where Christians gather to sing and praise the memory of the champion over death. These reflections are an appeal to keep the initiatory rites focused within the context of this greater memory and the authentic depth of the mystery of Christ, while at the same time maintaining a balance of taste and liturgical aptness in the celebration of the Mother of All Vigils.

Notes

1. If both adults and children are to be initiated at the Vigil, I would primarily use the texts for adults and accommodate the necessary elements according to the needs of the children. This adaptation is hinted at in the National Statutes at the end of the rite, no. 18.

2. For example, Gabe Huck, *The Three Days* (Chicago: LTP); Rupert Berger and Hans Hollerweger, eds., *Celebrating the Easter Vigil* (New York: Pueblo Publishing Co., 1983). See also William Reiser, S.J., *Renewing the Baptismal Promises* (New York: Pueblo Publishing Co., 1988); Rachel Reeder, ed., *Liturgy: Easter's Fifty Days* (3:1), *Putting on Christ* (4:1), and *Central Symbols* (7:1) (Washington, DC: The Liturgical Conference).

3. The Liturgy of the hours offers an example of the way this text could be used and built on. The antiphon appears from Holy Thursday evening prayer through Holy Saturday morning prayer, but it is not merely repeated. Each time it is added to. So on Holy Thursday we sing, "For our sake Christ was obedient, accepting even death." That is repeated on Good Friday with a small addition: " . . . accepting even death, death on a cross." On Holy Saturday the antiphon is completed: " . . . death on a cross. Therefore God raised him on high and gave him the name above all other names."

4. [Editor's Note] Some of them have already been set by several composers. See Chapter Twelve in this volume.

5. Note that if the reception alone is to be celebrated, a much simpler ritual outline is used, though it would have to be adapted for use in the Vigil. This outline is found in the RCIA, nos. 487–498. Some liturgists, the present author included, believe that if baptism is not celebrated at the Vigil, receptions into full communion alone make no sense. There is, in fact, no separate outline in the RCIA to show how to include receptions alone at the Vigil, suggesting that another time for receptions should be considered, as directed in the National Statutes for the Catechumenate (RCIA, Appendix III). Although receptions can occur "for pastoral reasons" at the Vigil when there are baptisms as well, "it is preferable that reception into full communion not take place at the Easter Vigil lest there be any confusion of such baptized persons with the candidates for baptism . . . " (Statute 33, see no. 34 as well). The

preferred time for such reception is at the parish community's Sunday eucharist, for the reason given in Statute 32.

6. Such an acclamation should be carefully chosen, however, so that it avoids disparaging baptism in other Christian communions and the candidates' previous faith journey and in no way hints at "triumphalism in the liturgical welcome into the Catholic eucharistic community" (National Statutes, no. 33).